Dedicated to all who
played the game, and
to the loyal fans
who supported them.

BOISE BASEBALL

The First 125 Years

Arthur A. Hart

Historic Idaho, Inc.

HISTORIC IDAHO, INC.
Boise, Idaho
1994

This book was published with the
generous assistance of West One Bank

Designed by Arthur A. Hart
Printed in the United States of America
by Joslyn-Morris Co., Boise, Idaho

Library of Congress Cataloging-in-Publication Data
Hart, Arthur A., 1921-
Boise Baseball: The First 125 Years / Arthur A. Hart
Library of Congress Catalog Card No. 94-76917

ISBN 0-9631258-6-9

Foreword

As a player, broadcaster, and fan of baseball in this area for more than 50 years, I have often wished for a book that covered the history of Boise's part in our great national pastime. Here it is, at last, with stories of some of the great players and interesting characters, and the many yarns that Arthur Hart has collected through years of research, and interviews with former players and those closely connected with the game.

Speaking personally, I especially enjoyed Arthur's treatment of the classy and fast Class C Pioneer League in which I played from its opening day in 1939. For me, it brought back a host of memories — of some of the finest minor league ball parks anywhere, like our own Airway Park, later Braves Field; of the fine big leaguers for which the Pioneer League was the spawning ground. I especially remember men like Larry Jansen who pitched for the Salt Lake Bees in 1940, and went on to a nine-year career with the New York Giants. We had at least one umpire who moved up to the majors — Augie Donatelli, who had a 23-year career in the National League.

And how about the two great right-handed pitchers from this area who had outstanding big league careers? Vernon Law from Meridian with the Pittsburgh Pirates, and Larry Jackson from Boise, with the St. Louis Cardinals, Chicago Cubs and Philadelphia Phillies. I also recall exhibition games we played at old Airway Park when Pittsburgh and Milwaukee came to town. Many other memories came back as I read Arthur's manuscript — the $1.25 per day meal allowance we had in the late Thirties and Forties; Class C league salaries of $100 to $135 per month, and those bus trips! Lewiston to Salt Lake City in 1939 was rough, but Boise to Billings in 1948 was just as bad.

Baseball has been part of the Boise scene, through good times and bad, for more than a century. This book captures the spirit of the game and the times in a warm and nostalgic way. The author knows the game and how to write about it.

WALT LOWE

BOISE, 1994

Introduction

I grew up in a western Washington family that loved the game of baseball. My mother was as avid a rooter for the home team as my father, brother and I were. My sister, I recall, was less enthusiastic than the rest of us, but in her later years rooted for the Seattle Mariners and watched them on television.

For as long as I can remember there was something deeply satisfying, esthetic as well as physical, about swinging a bat and connecting with a baseball. When you timed it just right and met it squarely, there was a surge of pure pleasure, from the point of contact, through the grain of the wood to your hands, through your arms to your chest. One could almost say, to your heart. I suppose everybody who ever played the game knows the feeling — hard to describe, but so wonderful.

Running down and snagging a fly ball, or scooping up a grounder and throwing to first, all in one fluid motion — these were esthetic as well as physical pleasures too. To paraphrase Oscar Hammerstein's *South Pacific* lyric — there is nothing like the game! And, it is America's game — a game of such splendid balance, requiring such varied skills, and played on a field of such ideal dimensions, that very little has had to be changed in 100 years. It is still 90 feet to first base and still 60 feet-six inches from the pitcher's rubber to home plate. Artificial surfaces, playing at night under the lights, and more scientifically designed equipment has actually had very little effect on the balance between offense and defense.

When we go back to the beginning of baseball in Boise, of course, it *was* a different game, but it is surprising how short a time it took for it to evolve into today's superbly proportioned "game of inches."

This is a book about baseball in Boise, Idaho, and primarily about players and teams that have represented the city in organized leagues, whether amateur, semi-professional, or professional. It includes, therefore, town teams from Oregon, Washington, Montana and Utah, as well as from Idaho. It does not include high school, college, or American Legion baseball, as worthy and interesting as those are. That would be another book.

ARTHUR A. HART

Contents

Bloody Noses and Disjointed Thumbs

Baseball was played in Boise as early as 1868, but it was a very different game from the one played today. Perhaps its most conspicuous feature was that the pitcher tossed the ball underhand from a box only 45 feet from the batter, rather in the manner of a softball pitcher, but without much speed. Even though it was legal for the pitcher to take a running start before delivering the ball as in cricket, his job was not to strike out the batter, but to toss the ball where he could hit it. The batter could even request the kind of pitch he wanted — high, low, or medium.

The baseball used in the 1860s was not as hard as the modern ball, and not yet standard in size, but it was plenty hard enough for fielders playing bare-handed on a rough dirt surface. Every hop of the ball was liable to be a bad hop. The ball was made of wound yarn with a stitched leather cover. The bat was flat on one or both sides and was called in early Boise a "paddle." Not until 1893 were all bats required to be round.

With the pitcher just putting the ball into play, allowing the batter to hit it as hard as he could, fielders had a real challenge. When the Boise Pioneer Base Ball Club was organized in March, 1868, the *Idaho Tri-weekly Statesman* predicted success for the effort, "as a means of amusement and healthful exercise," but warned that "bloody noses, disjointed thumbs, and cracked shins" could be expected. A call to practice in 1869 included this warning: "Sore hands no excuse."

After several weeks without a practice or a game in the summer of 1869, the *Statesman* asked "What has become of the Capital Club? Supposing it is warm; so much the better opportunity for the display of endurance as well as skill." Club secretary C. D. Vajen replied in humorous vein: "It was thought advisable to rest for several weeks to give the wounded a chance to recover. Oldham's nose, Riley's hand, and Logan's finger have all recovered without amputation."

Endurance was needed to play baseball in Boise during those first 20 years, not only because of summer heat, but because the rules made games long. It took nine balls to walk a batter, for example, and there were usually far more errors than hits. This made for long innings and incredibly high scores. A runner who advanced from first to third on a hit or an error was given credit for a stolen base. A ball that landed fair in the infield but bounced or rolled foul short of first or third bases was considered fair. Batters with skill learned to slice bunts wickedly so the ball landed just fair, then spun away from fielders into foul ground. On the other hand if a fielder could catch a foul ball on the first bounce it was an out.

Boise's early teams included some very prominent citizens. Thomas E. Logan, appointed postmaster by Abraham Lincoln in 1864, was an active member of the 1868 Pioneer Club and the 1869 Capital Club. He was elected mayor of the city four times over the next few years. Charles Himrod, president of the Capitals, was mayor in 1869 when the club issued a challenge to "any other nine that may be or may hereafter come into existence in this Territory." If the challenge was accepted there is no record of it, so it seems likely that intra-squad games were the rule in the late 1860s.

Those first baseball games in Boise were played where Idaho's capitol stands today. Called in 1869 "the public square," and later "capitol square," this two-block area, bounded by Sixth and Eighth, State and Jefferson, was a stretch of raw sagebrush desert that had to be cleared of "brush and rubbish" each spring before any games could be played.

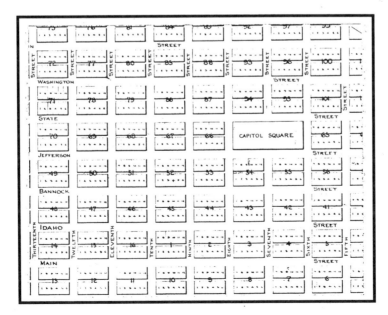

This early plat of Boise City shows the location of Capitol Square.

The Boys In Blue

Although a number of baseball teams were formed in Boise during the 1870s, including the public school Dodgers of 1875 who played the Capitals, the most important feature of the decade was the intense rivalry between town teams and soldier teams from Fort Boise. The Fort and the town had grown up together since 1863 and knew a lively interaction in social life that was occasionally antagonistic but generally friendly. The little frontier town of the Sixties and Seventies felt it needed the military post for protection, and the men at the Fort enjoyed the pleasures of the town as an escape from the boredom and routine of army life.

"The Nationals of Idaho" was the highfalutin team name chosen by the young men of Boise City as they prepared to take on the soldiers on March 25, 1877. They were, noted the *Statesman*, "all of splendid physique and powers of endurance, but wanting in the practice and familiarity with the game which distinguishes the veterans of Fort Boise." That day, "on the plain near the Fort," the locals were painfully humiliated by the soldiers' Eastern Rock club 61-18. Mercifully, no box score was kept but we can be sure that there were many more errors than hits. The Boise boys needed that "endurance" just to chase the ball around the outfield all afternoon.

Boise and Fort Boise were close neighbors and natural baseball rivals.

The local "Nationals" of 1877 no doubt took their name from the National League of Professional Base Ball Clubs, formed in New York in 1876. It was the first major league, and is, of course, still going strong today. (The American League was not fully established until 1903 when the first World Series was played.)

Baseball historians agree that errors were the most notable feature of the game in its early years, at the professional as well as the amateur level. It was during the 1870s that standard rules were adopted, and players began notably to raise their skills. Most of the strategies that are part of the game today, such as holding the runner at first, the sacrifice bunt, relaying throws from the outfield, and changing speeds on pitches, were developed in the 1870s.

Readers of the *Idaho Tri-weekly Statesman* of July, 1870, were given a glimpse of professional baseball even before the National League was organized. "We notice that this popular game, frequently called 'the national game,' has again taken possession of the youths in the east, and they are nearly all on the bat. Some of the names adopted by the clubs are striking, if not peculiar: 'Red Stockings,' 'Blue Stockings,' 'White Stockings,' 'Dirty Stockings,' 'Fir Mountains,' 'Hay Makers,' 'Peeled Heels,' 'Silver Heels,' etc. The 'Red Stockings,' or 'Cincinnatis' are the acknowledged champions of the United States, and after a contest, would be of the world. We have seen these boys play, and can endorse everything said of them . . ." The locals liked striking names too. The Know-nothings and the Bummers played a game at the Fort in 1879, called after four innings with the Bummers leading 13 to 10. Later Boise teams would have such picturesque names as Lobsters, Clippers, Chicagos, Cherubs and Fruit Pickers.

The Fort and the frontier town had a close and mutual dependency.

11

For The Honor Of The Town

Baseball flourished in the 1880s in Idaho, and inter-city contests and talk of state championships began to be heard. The rules were changed several times, in the decade, with the number of balls for a walk gradually reduced from eight in 1880, to seven in 1882, to six in 1884, back to seven in 1886, five in 1887, and to four, at last, in 1889. This speeded up the game considerably. The pitcher's box was backed up from 45 to 50 feet from home plate, and by the late '80s overhand throwing was permitted. As pitchers were allowed to throw harder, strikeouts became more a feature of the game, even though for awhile batters were allowed four strikes.

FIELDER CATCHING A FLY.

Boise Barracks teams continued to outplay civilian talent in the Eighties. The opening game of 1883 was won by the soldiers 30 to 2. In 1884 a new Capital Base Ball Association was formed with an initial subscription in April of $150 from business supporters. D.P.B. Pride, an attorney from Maine who had come to Boise in 1881, and who held the post of Register of the U.S. Land Office, was elected the club's first president. He played first base for the Capital team that season. A series of games with the soldiers drew large crowds to the Barracks grounds, including "many of the fair sex." The Capitals sported new uniforms for the first time on August 31, 1884, in a game called after nine innings with the score 13 to 13. "Both sides showed a gratifying improvement in their fielding, which was, with but few exceptions, excellent," said the paper. The Army players were members of D Troop, U.S. Second Cavalry.

STOPPING A GROUNDER.

Earlier games that season had been a lot wilder. In games marked by many errors, the soldiers won 41-24 on August 17, and the Capitals 27-22 on the 22nd. On August 24th the boys in blue won 34-29. By the end of the season the Capital City club was improving, and the *Statesman* tipped its hat to team captains Garson of the soldiers and Pride of the civilians "for the excellent results of their discipline, as shown on this and previous occasions in the gentlemanly conduct and bearing of the players and the good order maintained throughout the games." This comment was a reaction to the bad reputation major league players were beginning to get for violence, bad language and bullying umpires. By the 1890s rowdyism on the diamond would be a national scandal.

The baseball drawings on these next few pages appeared in Century Magazine in October, 1889.

The first big series of inter-city games held in Boise was in October, 1884, when the Salt Lake City Blues came to town. The home team lost the first two games, but hung on to win the third 13-12 on October 9. As "numerous fair and elegantly attired ladies . . . showed their sympathy with the gallant Boise boys by the most enchanting smiles of approval," the locals pulled out the narrow victory. It was said that Captain D.P.B. Pride got so excited when Boise scored four runs in the first inning that he stuck the lighted end of his cigarette in his mouth.

Of the Salt Lake players, the newspaper commented, "The members of the 'Lord's anointed' base ball club were not only champion ball players but charming songsters and lady killers. They promenaded the streets of the city Wednesday evening, singing short soul-subduing melodies and ogling everything from a lamp post to a Chinese scow."

Capitol Square, where the earliest baseball in Boise was played, was a busy place in 1889 when the Territorial Capitol was built. Central School is at left. Ada County courthouse at right.

AN "OUT CURVE"—THE BEGINNING.

AN "OUT CURVE"—THE END.

When the Blues went on to Denver at the end of October to play a series with the Denver Athletics the *Statesman* carried a brief account of each game. The Salt Lake boys lost three straight, but the scores were close.

Hailey had an excellent baseball team in 1885, and there was great local interest in organizing a tournament to play for a mythical state championship. Pocatello and Shoshone had played at Shoshone on July 6, with the home team winning 22-13, but Hailey's Wood River team then beat Shoshone 17-11, and crowed loudly over it. The *Statesman* commented, "Our nine is not in practice, but we could give them a far better game than that, which considering the score and errors, is not a very creditable one." Shoshone tried hard to raise the money for a tournament in August, but finally gave up. Hailey and Pocatello said they would rather play in Boise anyway if the capital city could raise the money. Boise's team continued to practice hard, and games between the Capital club and the newly formed Chicagos were played regularly.

On September 17, after continued negotiations, the Oregon Short Line railroad, in an attempt to give the fund-raising efforts a boost, agreed to give the ball players from out of town quarter rates, and half rates to their fans. The local committee for arrangements included Thomas E. Logan, former mayor and leading merchant who had played on Boise's first team in 1868. Other prominent citizens in charge of the event were W. H. Nye, Joseph Perrault, H.B. Eastman and Fred Epstein. They announced that prizes would be awarded the top three finishers in the tournament, and that all clubs in Idaho Territory were invited to compete free.

RUNNING TO FIRST BASE.

SLIDING TO BASE.

Hailey's Wood River team played Boise's Capitals in the first game of the series on September 25, 1885, and won 15 to 10. The game was marked by many errors and "a slow, drizzling rain." The local Chicagos played the Capitals and lost 22-12. "While the game was being played a strong breeze prevailed which is known as a 'batter's wind,' as it came from directly behind the bat, very materially assisting the batter when a hit was made and working to the serious disadvantage of the fielders in handling the ball, as the dust raised was directly in their eyes." The Capitals then beat Wood River 9-8 in the second of the series between the two, but lost the rubber game and the "Championship of Idaho" 15-13.

In October, four Boise players went to Salt Lake City to play on an Idaho all-star team against the Utah all-stars. Utah won the first game of the series 8-6, but Idaho won the next two 13-9 and 12-11. This was the first meeting in the inter-state rivalry that led eventually to the establishment of the Utah-Idaho league of 1926, and its successor the Pioneer League of 1939.

Attempts to renew a series with Wood River and other Idaho towns in 1887 failed, since the necessary expense and prize money could not be raised. The soldiers at Boise Barracks continued to furnish the opposition for town teams as they had for many years, for as yet there were no leagues, and no regular tournaments. "Championships" were still decided among teams that played less than 20 games a year. It was amateur baseball played for the love of it, and for the honor of the town.

THE CATCHER.

Fourth of July parade, 1890.

Nineties Nines

Idaho became a state on July 3, 1890, and the next day a confident Pocatello club played in Boise for bragging rights of the 43rd star in the national flag. When the Pocatello challenge was received in early June, the *Statesman* thought "a lively baseball game between two good clubs would add largely to the excitement and hilarity of the occasion," and for the rest of the month the home team practiced hard. On June 28th the paper announced a meeting "to which every baseball crank in Boise is cordially invited." Officers were elected and uniforms that had been ordered from Chicago earlier were eagerly awaited. When they arrived, the snazzy new outfits had "white sateen shirts, gray pants, maroon stockings, white belts and caps trimmed with maroon stripes, and blue canvas baseball shoes."

Preparations for the big game were elaborate. "A number of fly tents will be put up, under which those present may rest and watch the game with pleasure. The grounds will be leveled off and the necessary lines marked with whitewash to conform strictly to the rules governing the National League of ball players."

A month earlier a copy of *The Universal Baseball Guide,* edited by John C. Eckeland and Frank Connelly, published by Rand McNally of Chicago and New York, had arrived at Pinney's bookstore. The *Statesman* proclaimed it "a model of neatness," and said its usefulness lay in the complete set of National League playing rules for 1890 it contained, and "important information" from "prominent baseball players, stars in their particular positions."

A concession for "the privilege of selling lemonade, etc., at the game," was awarded, and S.E. Meyer was named to "perform the arduous duties devolving upon him as umpire." A local strong man bet he could throw a baseball farther than anyone in the state for $10 a throw.

A wire arrived from a Pocatello booster on July 2 giving the schedule of arrivals for his team, and advised, "Bet your last dollar on us, and you will either get rich or go broke." As it turned out, nobody did either and a good time was had by all. The final score, when the game was called after 10 innings, was 27 to 27.

A great inter-town rivalry developed that summer that would continue well into the 20th Century. Weiser and Caldwell had especially fine teams in the Nineties, and both would belong to some of the leagues in which Boise played for the next 40 years. Travel between rival towns was by railroad in those days and the Oregon Short Line offered special excursion rates for boosters. When the Boise team traveled to Weiser later in July, 1890, "On the way down the boys amused themselves by

Streetcars began running out Warm Springs Avenue in 1891.

17

*An early Weiser team —
not all had uniforms.*

trying to find a seat and keep cool." Of the game, won by Boise 21-7, the *Statesman* said, "Boyakin's curves were not solved by the Weiser batters."

Pitchers were now throwing harder, with more deception, but from only 50 feet away. (Not until 1893 was the rubber moved back to 60 feet 6 inches from home plate, as it is today). Bases were 90 feet apart then, as now, and it seems that the game had achieved ideal dimensions, despite all the later changes — bigger, stronger and faster players, a livelier ball, and artificial surfaces. Offense and defense have maintained a remarkably close balance in what is still "a game of inches."

In marked contrast to the rowdy reputation and crude behavior of professionals in the east, local amateur teams in the Nineties were friendly rivals. After Weiser beat Caldwell 21-8 in August, 1890, "they soothed the outraged feelings of their visitors with a free supper, and cheerfully promised to come up to Caldwell soon and repeat their performance. The Caldwell boys say they can't do it, and announce their determination to redeem their reputation or die. And some unpatriotic citizen has suggested that they had better order nine cheap coffins."

Caldwell lost the return game as well, but "The two nines became firmer friends than ever and the Caldwell boys say they would rather be beaten by Weiser than by any other nine on the Coast." After the game Caldwell hosted "a royal feast," and the town band played. "Several eloquent toasts and short speeches were given . . ." The *Weiser Leader* said "Long live the Caldwell boys, and may they defeat every nine (except the Weisers) that they may tackle." When Caldwell finally did beat Weiser 8-4 on September 28, the *Leader* said the Weisers didn't feel bad about it in the least. "Both nines played good ball and either of them can do Boise up, and Boise knows it and she gives them a wide berth." This kind of challenge via the press was common in the 1890s.

Attempts to form an Idaho-Oregon league in May, 1892, failed when the charge was made that La Grande had hired professionals. Caldwell withdrew, and Boise threatened to do so also if any team was not strictly amateur. At a scheduled meeting in Boise on May 24, 1892, Caldwell representatives came, but Boiseans didn't, using as an excuse that they were unable to raise enough money to support a team. Caldwell was understandably upset, and said that *they* could.

Boise did get a team together to play in Caldwell's new ball park on June 12, 1892, even though they could not commit to a league. The dedication ceremonies were held before a new 500 seat grandstand, and in the game that followed the Caldwell boys walloped the visitors 9-1. The *Statesman* reporter was impressed — not only with Caldwell's imposing facility and public support, but by the team's "neat uniforms of brownish gray with maroon trim." A rematch two weeks later was even more one-sided at 16-1. "Lack of practice lost the game for Boise," lamented the *Statesman*. Caldwell, on the other hand, enroute to what would be called later that year the State Championship, were "taking hold of baseball with a will . . . the finest grounds in the state have just been laid out . . ."

Caldwell's 1891 "Champions of Idaho" were darned proud of it. Standing: Will Maxey, James Flower, Jerry Kelleher, Dan Kelleher, Ed Hayes. Center: unknown; unknown; Charles Reed, manager; Hi Dunbar; Swain Beatty. In front: Hank Schwere and Captain Walter Sebree.

In 1893 Boise finally got its act together. By the Fourth of July the capital city team had beaten Caldwell three times in a row. There was no official Independence Day celebration in the city that year, due to the financial depression sweeping the country, but a large crowd attended the baseball game at the Natatorium field. Boise again defeated Caldwell 6 to 4.

When Idaho Falls brought a team to Boise for a three game set in August, 1893, the paper recorded the first as a "Remarkably Poor Game," with "many horrible errors on both sides." Boise had 27 runs, only 10 of them earned; Idaho Falls had 6, only 2 earned. Games #2 and #3 were just as bad — 14-2 and 41-7. The *Statesman* summed it up: "They are nice young fellows, but they can't play ball, and there is every reason to believe they will never again stray from their local pastures." ("Never again" is a long time, and Idaho Falls would have an outstanding record as a baseball town in the years ahead.)

Local baseball dominance had switched from Caldwell to Boise in 1893. Even the *Caldwell Tribune* was impressed: "Boise has a ball team to be proud of. After winning the championship of the state by beating Caldwell four straight games, they challenged the Portland, Oregon, nine and this week beat them unmercifully." Boise won the series with Portland two games to one, 7-6, 10-8, and 8-12, after which the *Statesman* reported of the Oregonians, "They are kickers from Kickville, but they can play ball." When Portland left on the train for a game at La Grande, young Boise fan Gwong Louie went along. "The versatile young Chinese known all over the city" had not yet returned when the *Statesman* expressed concern about his welfare. "Boise player Turner had him in charge, probably intended to bring him home after the game." Louie would continue to be a popular personality in Boise and an ardent baseball fan.

Every year in the Nineties a rite of spring was organizing a Boise baseball club all over again. This usually began with a public meeting of potential players and supporters. The teams were made up of amateurs who played for the love of the game itself,

This rare early action shot was taken at Emmett in about 1890.

21

but then, as now, special incentives and under the table cash were involved in keeping the best local athletes on the town team. The money collected from business supporters went primarily for uniforms, equipment and travel.

The national baseball picture was presented to *Statesman* readers in April, 1895, in a syndicated column called "Caylor's Ball Gossip" by one O.P. Caylor. He reported that nearly every state in the Union was now affiliated with a professional league and that enthusiasm for the game had never been higher. Idaho, of course, and Boise especially, being over 300 miles from the next large city was not included in any organized league, and did not have the population to support a professional team.

1895 was unique, Caylor reported, in that every one of the 12 National League teams was going south to train. Only Baltimore had done it before and its club won the 1894 championship. Rule changes adopted at league meetings that spring reflected concern over player conduct and the size of gloves.

New rules, "expected to curb the noisy catcher and completely squelch the unreasonable kicker," were hailed; "The kicking is hereafter confined to the two captains. If any private leaves his place in the field or the bench to question a decision he will be fined for the first offense and removed from the game. Indecent, obscene, or abusive language by a ball player on the field, whether applied to the umpire, a player, or a spectator, subjects him to a fine of from $25 to $100 and removal from the game." An umpire who failed to enforce these rules was also to be subjected to fines. "It follows that he will not fail in his duty."

"The glove and mitt rage has grown so much during the last year or two that some fears were felt that unless a check were given the fashion it would not be long before a baseball team going out to play would look much like soldiers of the Middle Ages on their way to battle." Only catchers and first basemen were to be allowed big mitts by the new rules, and the size of other gloves was severely limited. No doubt players and officials of the 1890s would be astonished at the gloves used today.

Caylor's syndicated column continued to run in the *Statesman* throughout the Nineties, and kept local baseball enthusiasts up to date on the latest developments in the professional game, even though there was very little action in Boise as the century neared its end. The hit-and-run strategy perfected by the Boston Red Sox was coming into fashion with other teams as well. Caylor reminded fans in 1896 that "the public marveled over the fact that the Bean Eaters could make more runs with fewer hits than any other team playing ball, and we heard a great deal about 'Boston luck.' It was not luck, but this system of 'hit and run.'" He also proved to be a prophet by advocating baseball clinics in the off-season by established stars, and the formation of farm systems by major league clubs.

The Fourth of July was always counted on to produce a baseball game as part of the festivities, but the tradition changed in the late 1890s. There were no July 4th games in 1897, 1898, or 1899. Instead, other sporting events took their place. Bicycling was the craze in the decade, and races at various distances became a standard feature of the Fourth. In 1896 there was also a pole-vaulting exhibition between local "experts," with the winner clearing 6 feet 5 inches! The last July 4 ball game of the decade took place in 1896 — a 5 inning affair between soldiers from the Barracks and local boys, won by the townies 7-5.

The Spanish-American War of 1898 called away Boise's best ball players, both soldier and civilian.

Departure of the Idaho Volunteers, 1898.

There was talk of a game to be played July 4, 1897, but it never materialized. Why did baseball go into such a decline in those years? The Spanish-American War, like all wars in our history, pushed baseball out of public concern. In Boise, where the military post had always supplied teams to rival those of the town, the war took away the best athletes from both groups. On April 22, 1898, Company A, Sixteenth Infantry, left by train for a southern mobilization point "amid waving banners and with the plaudits of a mighty throng ringing in their ears." A week later the Idaho Militia was mobilized at Boise from all over the state and was soon shipped south. After service in the Philippines, the Idaho Volunteers returned home at the end of September, 1899.

With baseball in temporary eclipse, cycling took over as Boise's leading sport. It was a craze shared by women as well as men, one observer estimating that by the end of the Nineties 40% of American women had bicycles.

This superb studio portrait shows a Weiser ball club, pre-Walter Johnson.

Play for Pay

At the turn of the century baseball in Boise was still an amateur game, but was beginning to turn semi-professional. Star athletes from one team were often hired to strengthen a second in a grudge match against a third. More was at stake than town pride, since games were often played for a purse, winner take all, and side betting was active. Professional baseball officially came to Idaho with Boise's entry into the Pacific International League in 1904, but for most of the first decade of the century only a few of the best players got paid.

Caldwell continued to be Boise's chief rival just as she had been in the Nineties. So many local rooters wanted to go to Caldwell for a game on June 23, 1901, that three box cars were pressed into service to haul them, after the three passenger cars allotted for the trip had been packed solid. The crowd, said the *Statesman*, was "the jolliest imaginable." They were all decked out with red ribbons, "official color of the Boise club." The Columbia Band added to the jollification, and when the train pulled into Caldwell a crowd was waiting to greet them. In the dramatic style of the day, the paper said, "Caldwell . . . held her breath [not knowing] that Boise had so many ardent admirers of baseball and of her matchless club."

After 1884, Idaho baseball teams traveled by train to games with rival towns.

Many games of the late '90s and early 1900s were played at the Natatorium field.

Less skilled teams made up of soldiers from Boise Barracks and town amateurs continued to draw local support, even when the city team played on the same day. The scores tell us the players were on a lower level than the town team. While Boise was beating a tough Caldwell nine 5-1, local amateurs were beating the soldiers 21-14. Fielding errors made the difference.

Two thousand fans turned out at the Natatorium field on June 16, 1901, to see a game between Pocatello and Boise, won by the locals 6 to 4. From the taunting tone of the *Statesman* coverage, one might suppose the game had been a slaughter instead of a clean, hard-fought close one: "To Pocatello — keep the head cool in really warm weather. Second — learn to play ball — get baskets; let your boys learn to wear roller skates; plug the holes in your bats; hire a hall and tell how it all happened." Admittedly, this may have been in response to similar taunts from Pocatello papers, but it lacked the spirit of good sportsmanship that was characteristics of the 1890s.

Boise continued to win in the 1901 season, even though other teams combined players in what were in some ways all-star combinations. Pocatello and Caldwell players joined Nampa for a game at the end of June but only added to the capital's seven-game win streak. The score was 4 to 2, with Boise getting two unearned runs off Nampa errors. Local enthusiasm is shown by the fact that the *Statesman* printed a play-by-play account of every game that summer, and by the fact that the very notion of amateurism was abandoned. There were regular reports of businessmen in rival towns coming up with money to get players able to beat Boise.

On July 1, 1901, the *Statesman* announced the arrival of Barney McQuade from Salt Lake City, "an old National League player." He may have been experienced, but official records fail to list him as ever having played even an inning of National League ball. In August it was announced that promoters Stone & Ramsdell were going to Portland for players, and that "all members of the old team have been paid off and released."

C. V. Stone and William Ramsdell, co-owners of the Natatorium ball park, tried hard to come up with a baseball team that Boise would support. After two losses to Baker on August 24th and 25th "owing to the failure to arrive of some of the new players from Portland and Spokane," and four road games in Utah, the season was pronounced finished.

The 1902 season began with the formation of a new Interstate League, probably so named because it had been hoped to get Oregon teams to join, although none did. Boise, Caldwell, Emmett and Nampa played under these rules: 12 players and one umpire made a team; admission was 50 cents for grandstand, 25 cents for bleacher seats; the winner got 60 percent of the gross, the losers 40 percent. Enthusiasm was great at first, as indicated by a turnout of 2,000 fans who saw Boise beat Caldwell 13-5 on May 11, 1902. A railroad excursion to a game with Emmett in June drew 250 Boise fans.

Since the league team played ball at the Natatorium field, the owners of Riverside Park decided to compete by forming a team of their own. "The players are all under salary," explained the *Statesman* on July 3, 1903, "and therefore must attend to the business of playing ball. Three players have been brought up from Salt Lake, and they are the pick of the ball tosser of the Utah town." This, as far as can be determined, was Boise's first all-professional team, although not part of a sanctioned professional league. The Riverside team thereafter played league teams at the park, and eventually replaced the town's semi-pro nine. Riverside Park drew 2,000 people on a good day, but with the arrival of the heat in August was getting only a few hundred.

The barnstorming New England Bloomers came to Boise on August 3, 1902, and played a game against local amateurs called

SUNDAY

BALL GAME

Aug. 3 Only.

New England Bloomers
vs.
Riverside Park

The Eastern Girls against the Western Boys in a red hot game.

The Bloomers' famous pitcher Miss Grace Wood, will positively appear in the box.

---

the Lobsters. It was advertised as "The Eastern girls against the Western boys in a red hot game," but turned out to be what the paper panned as "rotten," "very punk," and a "humbug." The Bloomers, augmented by a male shortstop and a male catcher, won 10 to 9. The reporter was not amused by the performance. "It will probably be many years before the people of Boise will allow themselves to be so shamefully 'faked' again. There might be some excuse for the 'exhibition' if the members of the team from New England (?) were even fairly good looking. Those who remained away from the park have every reason to be shaking hands with themselves."

A short-lived Idaho League was formed in 1903, but folded on June 23 when Caldwell was forced to disband for lack of support. Exhibition games to help raise money for players who hadn't been paid enough to get back to their home cities continued until July 6, when it was admitted that "the season proved a costly experiment . . . every club being considerably out of pocket. Boise turned out the only paying crowds, yet the team disbanded nearly $500 to the bad." The conclusion drawn was that "the Idaho public is too busy to attend ball games," and that church opposition to Sunday games kept many away.

Boise's first venture into a recognized professional baseball league came in 1904 when veteran promoter and baseball legend "Honest John" McCloskey came to town to manage the Fruit Pickers in the Pacific International League. He had founded the Texas League in 1887 and had managed teams at Sacramento, Houston, Montgomery, Savannah, Louisville, Dallas, Montgomery, Great Falls and Tacoma before becoming a founder of the new Pacific International in 1902 at Butte, where he led the Miners to the championship. Always moving, McCloskey managed San Francisco in 1903, when that team was still in the league, and came to Boise in 1904 when what had been an eight-team league in 1903 was reduced to four. The great travel distances by train, when the league included Los Angeles, San Francisco, Portland, Tacoma, Butte, Helena and Salt Lake City, caused most of the teams to lose money. The Portland franchise switched to Salt Lake City in mid-1903.

In the league's last season, 1904, "Honest John" led the Boise Fruit Pickers to the championship with a record of 82-49, .626. The Spokane Indians were second, Butte Miners third, and Salt Lake Elders last. McCloskey earned popularity in Boise for his ability to inspire young players, and for his insistence on clean living and physical conditioning. When Spokane's owner wanted another crack at Boise after the regular season ended, he offered to bet "a cool thousand" that his team could win a five-game series from Boise at Spokane. The *Statesman* said, "Honest John is known to be unalterably opposed to betting of any kind, whether upon the result of a game, the result of a series of games, or a pennant race. He holds that betting debases the great American game, which is conceded to be the cleanest sport on earth."

The Southern Idaho League

Boise fielded an amateur team in 1905 that had success against the town teams of Caldwell, Nampa, Meridian and Mountain Home, but having had a taste of professional league baseball, the city's fans were eager to get back into faster company. In September, Boise and Butte, whose teams had played in the Pacific International League in 1904, applied for franchises in the Northwest Baseball League. The negotiations fell through, and in the spring of 1906 Boise helped organize the Southern Idaho

League with teams from Caldwell, Emmett, Nampa, Payette and Weiser. This was a semi-professional league, with only a few of the top men getting paid.

When Boise played at Weiser on May 20, 1906, the feature of the game that got all the press in Weiser's 17-1 victory was the emergence of a local farmer as the team's star catcher. He got dubbed "Foxy Grandpa" that day after a flawless performance behind the plate. "There was a time, so the old timers in the baseball world assert, when Foxy Grandpa used to play ball regularly. But some 15 years ago or so, he felt his bones stiffening and the rheumatics would come on when the wind was howling around the house at night, and he concluded to stop the strenuous life. He moved out to sunny Idaho and established himself on a farm near Weiser.

"Just as a reminder of the old times, Foxy Grandpa went to town last Sunday and saw the game between Boise and Weiser at the Washington County town. He was disgusted to think the Weiser team would be beat by such an aggregation as that from the capital.

"'Huh,' he said, 'I am old and fat and grey headed, but I can play ball enough to beat that bunch.'" Foxy Grandpa, whose name was Miller, made no errors, threw out a runner, drew a walk, made a base hit, scored two runs and even stole a base. A week later he was again Weiser's star as his team pounded Payette 12-0. "He made a sensational long hit and although he is not shaped for a sprinter, he reached third on it." Miller helped Weiser so much that other teams began to complain that he was a professional.

Though not a member of the Southern Idaho League, Baker City was a natural Boise competitor, since the two teams were about the same size and connected by the Oregon Short Line Railroad. When Boise defeated Baker 8-2 in June, 1906, the *Statesman* was gracious about the visitors. "The entire team made friends of everyone at the park because, while they were beaten, they played clean, honest, and honorable ball — no horse-play or Billingsgate." (Billingsgate: coarse and abusive language.)

Caldwell won the short Southern Idaho league season that ended on the Fourth of July. Walter Sebree, a fine athlete who made his living as a banker, had starred on Caldwell town teams since 1890, playing a variety of positions including first base and pitcher. Most of those years he had been both organizer and manager of Caldwell teams. His prestige was such that Boise tried unsuccessfully to hire him as manager in 1901.

The second season of 1906 began after Boise's Riverside park management arranged for a game every Sunday between valley teams. Weiser boasted on July 8 that they had the best team in the league just finished, despite Caldwell's record. "Kid Johnson is regarded here as the greatest pitcher in Idaho." Boise hadn't seen him yet, but in 1907 they would become believers. The 1906 season ended in mid-August. Boise's managers stated that gross receipts from admissions were $1500 and total expenses $1000. Of the latter, 15% of the gate had gone for rental of the Riverside field.

The Idaho State League

If it had no other claim to fame, the Idaho State League would be memorable for having sent Walter Johnson directly to the big leagues in the summer of 1907. Even though some baseball historians have written that the great Washington Senators pitcher made the majors "without having spent a day in the minor leagues," that is only true because the Idaho State League was semi-professional, and not eligible to join the National Association of Professional Baseball Leagues, governing body of the minors.

As a matter of fact, the Idaho State League, successor to the Southern Idaho League of 1906, was made up of a colorful and highly competitive group of teams representing most of the towns in southwest Idaho. And what wonderful names they had — Boise Senators, Caldwell Champions, Emmett Prune Pickers, Mountain Home Dudes, Nampa Beet Diggers, Payette Melon Eaters, Weiser Kids, and one Oregon team, the Huntington Railroaders. Only Emmett was not on the Oregon Short Line main line, but had been connected to it since 1901 by Col. William H. Dewey's Idaho Northern. Since teams and their fans traveled to games by train in those days, transportation linkage was vital to a league's success.

The 1907 season was a short one, with nearly all games played on weekends. This allowed a hard-throwing youngster like Walter Johnson to pitch most of the games the Weiser Kids played. On May 5 he shut out Nampa and struck out 14. On May 12 at Mountain Home the game was called after an inning and a half with Johnson behind 3-0 after allowing one hit followed by two errors by his teammates. The dust was so bad spectators couldn't see the players, and Johnson's infielders couldn't see the ball. May 20 a large Boise crowd went to Weiser to see their players go "down before the mighty Johnson like grass before a reaper." He allowed one hit and struck out 19 in a game that

Walter Johnson in a Weiser uniform, 1907.

lasted only an hour and 20 minutes. The *Statesman* said, "Johnson is undoubtedly in a class of his own and no pitcher in Idaho can approach him in speed and deceptive curves." On May 27 he threw another shutout, and struck out 10.

About this time the papers began to notice that his string of scoreless innings was beginning to mount. June 2 he allowed one hit, no walks, and struck out 14. This made it 48 innings without a run, and ran his strikeout total to 127 in 72 innings. By June 9 it was 57, and on the 15th, 66. The *Statesman* reported on June 18, 1907, that Walter Johnson had received an offer from the Washington Senators, a team called "hapless and hopeless" at the time. For years an oft-repeated quip was "Washington — first in war, first in peace, and last in the American League." The team needed help and 1907 was the year they got it. Washington catcher Cliff Blankenship, who was out of the lineup with a broken finger, was sent west to take a look at Johnson. Pongo Joe Cantillon, Senators manager, had already received a series of letters from Idaho extolling the talents of Weiser's strikeout king. This one is often quoted in baseball histories:

> You better come out here and get this pitcher. He throws a ball so fast nobody can see it and he strikes out everybody. His control is so good that the catcher just holds up his glove and shuts his eyes, then picks the ball, which comes to him looking like a little white bullet, out of the pocket.

> He's a big, 19-year-old fellow like I told you before, and if you don't hurry up someone will sign him and he will be the best pitcher that ever lived. He throws faster than Addie Jones or Amos Rusie ever did, and his control is better than Christy Mathewson's. He knows where he's throwing because if he didn't there would be dead bodies strewn all over Idaho. So you'd better hurry, Joe, or you'll be sorry.

On June 29, 1907, *The Washington Post* and *Idaho Statesman* both ran the story of Johnson's signing with the Senators. The day before, he had pitched another shutout, running his scoreless streak to 75 innings. The *Post* story was enthusiastic but exaggerated, claiming that Johnson *averaged* 20 strikeouts a game. It was actually about 16, and that was phenomenal enough.

On June 30, after having pitched the day before, the 19-year-old kid from California showed he was durable, as well as fast and accurate. He pitched shutout ball against Caldwell for 10 in-

The Emmett Prune Pickers of 1907. They battled "the mighty Johnson."

nings, only to lose 1-0 in the 11th when an error let in a run. The streak ended at 85 innings.

Five thousand people came to Boise's Riverside Park on July 4, 1907, to see the great one, already on his way to the American League. This time it was Campbell, Boise Senator's pitcher, who lost a heart-breaker on an error. Each pitcher allowed but three hits; Johnson struck out 10, Campbell 13; final score 2-1. It was the only time that season that anybody outdid Johnson in the strikeout department. After Johnson tripled over the centerfielder's head in the second inning Campbell struck out the side — one reason Boise fans could claim that their man had outpitched the mighty Johnson.

Just how great was Walter Johnson? A major baseball encyclopedia rates him the greatest of all time, basing its decision on a complicated computer-crunching of the statistics — wins and losses, earned-run average, quality of the opposition, quality of the team supporting him, and so on. His 110 shutouts lead all major league pitchers, and no active player is even close. Roger Clemens' 34 is tops today, and Nolan Ryan finished with 61. This calculation rates Johnson first, Cy Young second, and Lefty Grove third. Clemens rates ahead of all active pitchers, at 14th.

Walter Perry Johnson, "The Big Train," was born in Humboldt, Kansas, and came from California to pitch in Idaho. He spent the rest of his life in Washington, D.C. where he died December 10, 1946, but Idaho will always claim him. After all, it was here that he first showed the world that he could pitch.

The Caldwell champions and Mountain Home Dudes paraded through Mountain Home on opening day, 1907. The town band played, the crowd followed.

The regular season of 1907 ended with Weiser in first place by half a game over Caldwell, and one game over Boise. Mountain Home, fourth, was convinced that it could beat Weiser in a special series. Owner J.H. Garrett and manager E.T. Goddard challenged Weiser to a three game set — each side to put up $2500, winner take all. Walter Johnson, playing first base for Weiser in the first game, played errorless ball and got three base hits. His team won 6-1. Weiser made it three straight when Johnson out-pitched his Fourth of July rival Campbell, this time pitching for Mountain Home. Walter struck out 13 and held the Dudes scoreless.

The practice of "loading up" for a game on which heavy bets had been placed was exemplified in a game between Payette and Caldwell on July 7, 1907. Payette hired Walter Johnson and five other Weiser players to go against the Champions. Caldwell had loaded up against Weiser a week earlier and won, so the Weiser players enjoyed the 4-2 outcome. "Honors between Steitz, the Caldwell pitcher, and Johnson were about even, but Steitz was handicapped by not having a catcher who could hold him . . . four times he lost strikeouts because Foster, the former Senator, could not hold the last strike." We are reminded that Walter Johnson never had that problem at Weiser. True, his control was exceptional but he must have had a pretty good catcher as well to handle those blazing fast balls.

A new four-team Idaho State League was organized at the end of July, 1907, to continue play. A constitution and by-laws were adopted, including a ban on teams borrowing players and loading up. "It was this work that made the closing season of the eight-team league almost a disgrace and injured baseball to some extent," commented the *Statesman*. The four towns wanting to continue were Weiser, Boise, Nampa and Caldwell, but interest among fans was lukewarm. The last game of the season was won by Boise's ace Campbell. He allowed only one hit, struck out 8, and shut out Weiser 5-0. With Walter Johnson on his way to Washington, the Kids were not the same team. He had almost single-handedly pitched them to the 1907 pennant.

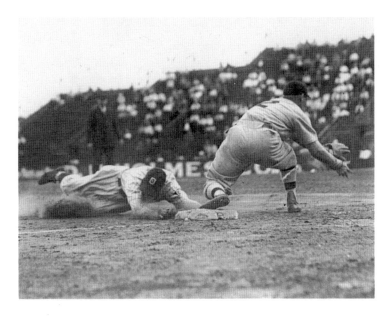

Safe at second.

Base Ball

Greatest matched games of ball in the
West in years for $5,000

$2500 A SIDE

Mountainhome vs. Weiser

THE DATES AND PLACES

Saturday, July 13 at Weiser

Sunday, July 14 at Boise

Monday, July 15 at Boise

Do not miss these games. They will be
great diamond battles

*This ad appeared in
the* Idaho Statesman,
July 7, 1907.

The Boise Valley League

Two amateur leagues played in Boise in 1908. The long-standing inter-town rivalry was continued in the Boise Valley League, and a Twilight League made up of teams sponsored by local businesses competed on summer evenings after work. Although both leagues were billed as "amateur," the old practice of beefing up a team with veterans of semi-pro ball created quite a fuss. The Bell Telephone team hired two men from Weiser's 1907 champs, technically eligible as long as they were employees of the company. Other teams protested, but had to play the "Blue Bells" anyway. When the phone company won the silver cup, symbolic of the championship in August, the *Statesman* called it a tarnished accomplishment. Boise & Interurban streetcar men finished second and the Bankers third.

The Boise Valley League was made up of the Boise Shamrocks, Boise Athletics, Middleton, Meridian, Nampa and Star. The Shamrocks won the title.

Nightwatch in a Morgue

A *Statesman* reporter said of the 1909 season, "Writing baseball in Boise is almost as joyful a job as being the nightwatch in a morgue. With both of the city's teams so far in the cellar they can never get out, it's anything but pleasant to tell how it all happened."

Boise fielded a team in the semi-pro Intermountain League in 1909, competing with the Butte Miners, Helena Senators, and Salt Lake Mormons. Helena won in a close race with Salt Lake, and Boise's Irrigators finished a distant last.

The Boise Shamrocks played in a revived Idaho State League and finished with an even worse record than the Irrigators. Nampa won over Caldwell, Emmett, and Boise, and went on to play Pocatello for the Championship of Idaho. They lost three straight games in September, and a generally unsatisfactory season for Boise rooters was over.

Idaho City lost an August game to Placerville 20-2, after which the *Idaho World* complained that Chinese musical instruments and a large cowbell had contributed to the defeat.

Hardware Men

Boise was well represented in the 1910 season by a semi-pro team sponsored by Jim Lusk's Carlson-Lusk Hardware Co. Veteran pitcher Campbell played for Caldwell that year, and handled an outfield position when not on the mound. The hardware men and Caldwell split two games over the Fourth of July weekend. The Twilight League had a successful season, but after 30 games decided to call it quits on July 23. President C.F. Easter said it was because of "varied amusements now to be enjoyed in the city and the great heat." He added that, "The league was organized solely for the recreation and pleasure of members as well as to give some pleasure to fans of the city, and when playing became a burden it was decided by unanimous consent to discontinue for the season. Any games which are played by any of these teams at any time from now on until the close of the summer will not be under the league, which does not believe in Sunday ball games or in money games. The members may indulge in such games as individuals, but the league has been disbanded . . ."

Caldwell's Recreation Park hosted its first baseball game in April, 1910.

Carlson-Lusk played a game with Payette on August 9, 1910, before going to Hailey for a six-day tournament among what were billed as the "fast teams" of southern Idaho. Blackfoot stopped in Twin Falls for a double-header on the way to the tournament and lost both games before a crowd of over 1,000 people. Three hundred Blackfoot rooters had come by train to back their team. The Oregon Short Line, as usual, gave fans an excursion rate. Carlson-Lusk beat Hailey 8-2 in the first game, then lost to Twin Falls 3-0. Next day the Boise team pounded Jerome 13-1. By winning two games from Twin Falls on August 24, Boise was declared to have won the tournament and "championship of the state."

Idaho Falls, which had been scheduled for the Hailey games, but unable to make it, was then booked into Boise's Riverside Park for a Labor Day series with Carlson-Lusk. Jack Vining held the visitors to six hits to win the first game 4-2. Idaho Falls slaughtered Boise pitching and won 11-2 in the second, and won the third 2-1. Idaho Falls took the best-of-five series on Labor Day when they won the second game of a double header. It was now the eastern Idaho team's turn to declare themselves champions of Idaho.

The Union Association

Honest John McCloskey, who had led Boise to the championship of the Pacific National League in 1904, was instrumental in organizing another Class C League in 1911. In November, 1910, he wrote to S.W. Cody of Boise urging him to rally support for a Boise entry in the new Union Association, scheduled to begin play in the spring. Cody, for whom an historic Boise ball park would be named, said, "The Union League should be a great success, as both McCloskey and [W.H.] Lucas, who is slated for president, are old ring horses of the Northwestern League, and, in fact, have practically made that organization what it is today."

Jack Cody put up $1600 of his own money for the Boise franchise, and the *Idaho Statesman* supported him in an April, 1911, article headed "Urgent Appeal is Made to Citizens to Support Boise Team in League." If Boise was not to lose the franchise Cody had paid for, money had to be raised to build a ball park. The local carpenters' union voted to work free if materials for a grandstand and bleachers could be found. The diamond itself, near the intersection of Warm Springs Avenue and Avenue C, had already been laid out and fences built. The team, made up of semi-pros and a few imported professionals, was practicing hard in early April for the season opener on the 25th. There was speculation as to what kind of team Honest John McCloskey would bring down from Butte for the first game with Boise's Irrigators. "The conclusion drawn from many a fanning bee is that Jawn has got another gang working out someplace, and that about April 25 he intends to ship in a bunch of live ones and take the locals by surprise." The Butte Miner lineup McCloskey had announced was not very impressive, and Boise fans were suspicious. "Now the Boise bunch savvy Jawn one long time, and they can't recall ever seeing him drive the morgue wagon."

McCloskey fielded a good team for the 1911 season, but the Miners finished third behind champion Great Falls and runner-up Salt Lake City. Former big-leaguer Cliff Blankenship, who had signed Walter Johnson for the Washington Senators in 1907, managed, caught, and played first base for the Salt Lake Saints. He stole home twice that season — the only one in the league to do it. Boise was fourth with a so-so .451 percentage and Helena and Missoula trailed.

The Western Tri-state League

The Class D Western Tri-state League played three seasons of professional baseball. Boise's Irrigators finished second to the Walla Walla Bears in 1912. The Pendleton Buckaroos were third and La Grande Pippins last. Carl Mays, Boise's star pitcher, set a league record by striking out 15 Pippins on August 1, 1912. He was clearly the class of the league. On June 30 the fireballing submariner hit Pendleton pitcher-manager Jesse Garrett in the head with a fast ball. The scrappy Garrett tried to continue to pitch but was not effective after that and Boise won. Carl Mays also hit Pendleton's center fielder with a pitch in the same game, and threw a wild pitch — indicative of his intimidating style and a foretaste of his future.

The grandstands at Cody Park burned to the ground on August 26, 1912 — a loss estimated at $7500. New bleachers were hurriedly put up and the season continued without interruption. The facility would continue to be known as Cody Park until replaced by Public School Field in 1925.

Baker, Oregon, and North Yakima, Washington, joined the league in 1913, but before the season ended La Grande and Baker had both been forced to drop out due to poor attendance and financial losses. When the season ended on September 7, 1913, Boise led North Yakima by five games and was declared winner. There was already strong sentiment in town for the team to switch back to the Union Association for the 1914 season, but there was some doubt that that league could continue either. The Montana teams had lost money and only Salt Lake City was able to draw crowds consistently.

Carl Mays

Carl Mays.

He was arguably one of the best pitchers of all time, yet he never made the Baseball Hall of Fame. He had a higher lifetime winning percentage than 15 pitchers who did, including Cy Young, Walter Johnson, Bob Feller, Bob Gibson, Tom Seaver and Warren Spahn. His name was Carl Mays, and he pitched phenomenal ball for Boise in 1912, winning 24 and losing 9 — best in the Western Tri-state League. Among his statistics that year, and in the 15 years he pitched in the major leagues, is one that accounts for a lifetime of unpopularity with opponents and the press — he hit lots of batters. The one-hit batsman that probably kept Mays from ever being considered for the Hall of Fame came in August, 1920, while he was pitching for the Yankees. One of his submarine fastballs hit Cleveland star Ray Chapman in the temple. He died the next day — the only major league player ever to be killed by a pitched ball. (A minor-leaguer named Will Traynor died in a game at Koshkonong, Wisconsin, on July 2, 1912, after he was hit near the heart by a fast ball.) Several big-league players had their careers shortened after being beaned: Mickey Cochrane, Ducky Medwick, Tony Conigliaro, and Dickie Thon, but only Ray Chapman was killed.

My father, who was a life-long baseball fan, believed to his dying day that Mays was "a dirty pitcher" who threw the "bean ball" far too often to maintain an edge over hitters, even though nearly all successful pitchers have used at least a "brush back" pitch as an accepted tactic to keep batters from getting too comfortable at the plate. It must be remembered that not until Mays' fatal beaning of Chapman were umpires required to keep a clean white ball in play. The one that killed Ray Chapman was dirty and grass-stained, was a submarine pitch that rose from an odd angle, and broke in on a right handed batter. Still, the perception continued among a large part of the public that Mays may have thrown at Chapman deliberately, and that he didn't seem sorry enough for what he had done. Ray Chapman was a likable young player, and Carl Mays was not.

In 1921, a year after the tragedy, Mays appeared in 45 games for the Yankees and led the American League with a record of 27-9. In 1926 he led the National League with 24 complete games for the Cincinnati Reds. His lifetime percentage of .622 equals that of Hall of Famer Carl Hubbell, and surpasses those listed above.

"Kill Him, Kill The Umpire"

Umpires today have control of the game on the field as they rarely did in baseball's early days. Top umpires are respected for their skill, judgement, and fairness, and some of them are as well known as top players. References to umpires in early Boise news accounts of games are common, and reflect the way they handled their jobs. They received praise occasionally, but were more likely to make the papers after what the home-towners regarded as bad calls.

"George H. Green umpired the game with great fairness" said the *Statesman* after a game between the Salt Lake City Blues and Boise's Capitals, played in October, 1884. In September, 1885, a Mr. Voris, who umpired the Territorial championship series between Wood River and the Capitals, "gave complete satisfaction, and the fairness and soundness of his judgment was universally commended."

Not so fortunate was a Mr. Goodwin of Bellevue, former publisher of the *Bellevue Press.* Calling him "the referee," the *Wood River Times* reported that "he made two decisions that the Haileyites claimed to be unfair, words followed, then blows, and the game broke up." This 1890 account doesn't say who dished out the blows or who received them, but there were apparently no arrests. That violence erupted over umpires' decisions was not uncommon is confirmed in the report of another 1890 game between Caldwell and Weiser: "A large crowd was present and witnessed the game, which went off in the most pleasant manner and was entirely free from *the disgraceful squabbles that usually mar the pleasure of the ball games.*"

Of a 1901 game, played in Boise at the Natatorium park between Baker City and the home club, the *Statesman* said, "George Bushnell umpired. The crowd thought he made several rank decisions, especially when he called Brookler out at third." The crowd's unhappiness with umpire Bushnell may have been aggravated by the fact that there were many bets being placed throughout the game, and that a bottle of whiskey was passed through the stands. Boise Manager Livingston said it was the last time liquor or bad language would be tolerated. "Such offenders in the future will be arrested and punished."

The *Statesman* defended umpire Bushnell's work in a game between Pocatello and Boise June 16, 1901. "What's the matter with Bushnell? Sometimes the rooters kick on his decisions, but all admit he is strictly fair. His calling Brookler out because the fellow was trying to 'play hoss' with the catcher was applauded by everyone. He wants the men to play ball. Good boy."

A new umpire, G.C. Porter, took the field on June 30, 1901, in a game between Nampa and Boise. He "got it good from the rooters when he first went into the field, but as he warmed up to it they forgave him in part. He really did make several decisions, though, that no one but an old hand at the business would have attempted." Porter got mentioned in the account of another Nampa-Boise game that season: "Roos made a small hit in the seventh, and a wild throw over first let him go on by. As he reached second the umpire woke up and told Roos he was out. It was the umpire with the goo-goo eyes who put him out. Roos laughed — so did everybody else."

Umpires had to defend themselves when players got out of hand, as in a game between Nampa and Payette on May 19, 1907. When umpire Jacobsen of Payette called one of the Payette players safe at first, Nampa's center fielder punched him. The crowd came to Jacobsen's defense and escorted him off the field.

Boise manager Tom Kotchman seems to be telling the umpire "He was out by a mile!"

Then, Nampa first baseman Collins ran over and hit the abused ump in the eye. This was one blow too many. Jacobsen broke loose from friendly fans and "soundly thrashed" Collins.

Boise's Union Association team of 1911 made many complaints about the umpiring, and the home-town *Statesman* newspaper backed them all the way. In May, "Frary's judgment the whole way around the field, and especially on balls and strikes, was rotten, and the peculiar part of it was that he always seemed to give the Boise team the worst of it . . ."

In July, the paper printed a letter from a prominent Boise supporter demanding that Union Association President Lucas fire umpire Rastus Wright, who, he claimed, was not giving Boise a square deal and "did not intend to." "How Lucas can expect to get fair decisions from a man who as a player was considered one of the greatest of boneheads, and who was always making trouble on his team, is more than anyone except Mr. Lucas can understand." Traditionally, league presidents hired the umpires and arbitrated disputes over rules, hence the attack on President Lucas.

During an August game at Helena the bleacher crowd swarmed onto the field after umpire Lawler made several questionable calls and then threw Helena Senators right-fielder Irby out of the game for arguing too long. Irby himself broke up what could have been an ugly situation by persuading the fans to go back to their seats. Boise Manager Kellackey protested the 7 to 6 loss because he had not been informed that a ball hit into the automobiles lining the outfield was a ground rule double. The ruling cost Boise a run, and maybe the game.

Even with strong backing from the league office umpires were often in trouble with emotional and partisan fans, and the newspapers delighted in recounting each incident. After a 1915 Idaho-Oregon League game between Ontario and Boise, in which an Ontario player was ejected, the *Statesman* said, "Umpire Kelleher was not in the best form . . . early in the game he got in wrong with both teams and the grandstand. He improved toward the last, and there were not many kicks registered during that session." A week later, "Umpire Jerry Kelleher was all to the bad, both on balls and strikes and on his base decisions. He stood far to one side of the pitcher's box and made no effort to cover the field on a play to the bases. In the seventh inning Friene was tagged out easily by a foot from the plate and was called safe. There were a number of others but of less consequence." It took a tough hide to be an umpire in that league with reporters picking at you constantly, but Kelleher apparently could take it. He continued to work games in Boise Valley for many years thereafter.

Mayor Marlin J. Sweeley of Twin Falls was brave enough to umpire balls and strikes in an exhibition game between major league all-star teams played in his town on November 9, 1915. The game was called at the end of nine innings with the score tied 4-4, and if the mayor made any controversial calls it was not reported.

The heat may have been a contributing factor in a 1923 game "marred by jangling with umpires." Two players suffered mild sunstroke and had to be revived. "At frequent intervals throughout the game, when either Danielson or Shonwald, umpires, made an apparently inaccurate decision, play was suspended until the differences were ironed out."

The grand old game will never be free of close calls, disputed by players and managers, but under today's league rules the umpire is boss. Evictions from the field end most arguments in a hurry. Being human, even the best umpires miss a call once in awhile, and don't mind admitting it, but their integrity is unquestioned, and their prestige generally high. Under all league rules today, players who are too demonstrative in disputing an umpire's call can be fined as well as evicted. Should they lose control so far as to push an umpire they can be suspended by the league president for as many games as the action warrants.

Has anyone ever killed an umpire during a game? Unfortunately, yes. Two minor league umpires died after being hit over the head with bats in the hands of players gone berserk after called strikes, but those were not in Idaho.

Andy Harrington, who managed the Twin Falls Cowboys in 1941, "discusses" an umpire's decision.

The Union Association — Round Two

The 1914 Union Association opened with Butte and Helena, Montana, Salt Lake, Ogden and Murray, Utah, and Boise, Idaho. The Salt Lake Seagulls won the first half of a split season. The Boise Irrigators were fifth, nine games back.

A feature of the *Idaho Statesman's* coverage of baseball that season was a gossipy column on the sports page headed "As Glimpsed from the Crow's Nest." It was full of short quips and observations on the games that fans must have enjoyed, such as "Once in awhile Joe Woods buzzed one over a la W. Johnson, but it was so seldom that he got 'em over." Woods had struck out six but walked nine in Helena's loss to Boise 6-5 on July 9, 1914. Other samples from the "Crow's Nest:" "When Jensen came in from left field after the fifth inning he went over to the bleachers and addressed a few remarks to a fan who had been panning him. Such stuff is all right for Ty Cobb, but Erve was hardly playing a Ty Cobb game . . . Longanecker (umpire) called for a policeman when he ordered McMurdo off the field. Officer Stadnik answered the call and before he left the field he challenged the whole Butte team . . . McMurdo climbed a telephone pole outside the park and saw the rest of the game from there . . . Holmes (a Boise substitute) has not been to the park for two days. He figures that as soon as he gets there Longanecker will chase him out, so he intends to save his carfare . . . If the explosion happens this will be your last chance to see a Union Association game."

The "explosion" was the interruption of the second half of the 1914 season after only a dozen games had been played. Boise dropped out of the league with a 5-7 record and third place in the standings. Murray also quit, leaving four teams to finish. The survivors drew for the use of Boise and Murray players for the balance of the season, although they remained the property of their home clubs for possible use in a reorganized league in 1915.

Boise Valley fans still wanted baseball, even though they had not supported the Union Association very well. One complaint, heard often in 1914, was that 75 cents for a grandstand seat, and 50 cents for the bleachers, was just too much and kept fans away. "The high prices have been attacked all over the circuit," said the *Statesman* on August 2, 1914. "They were mainly responsible for the poor support given the Boise team." League directors tried to save the season by instituting "25 cent bargain days," but it was too late for Boise.

The Trolley League

The answer, received with enthusiasm locally, was a "loop the loop" league, built around the Boise & Interurban streetcar line that had opened for business in 1907. The interurban linked valley towns in a loop that went out State Street to Eagle, Star, Middleton and Caldwell, and returned by way of Nampa and Meridian. Nampa and Caldwell were happy to renew the rivalry with Boise that went back to the 1890s. Two semi-pro teams sponsored by local businesses represented the capital in the new four-team league — Sweet-Teller Hardware at 900-902 Main, and Fred Murphey Cigar Store at 809 Main.

The opening game of the Trolley League season featured Nampa against Sweet-Teller at Nampa. "The crowd was probably the largest ever at Fisher's park, filling the grandstand and overflowing to the shade of the fences. Mayor Partridge pitched the first ball, sending it in the general direction of the grandstand; Chief of Police Molaney attempted to arrest its flight, and Dr. Kellogg, president of the league, was the receiving end of the battery."

Jack Wyman, star athlete from Boise High, held Nampa to one hit, struck out 16, and hit a long home run. On the following weekend it was Murphey's pitcher, Bersing, who made life miserable for Nampa. He gave up only two hits and pitched a shutout while striking out nine. A week later it was Bersing's turn to be outpitched. "Big Bill" Kuss, former Boise Irrigator pitcher, struck out 14 for Sweet-Teller. Nampa beat Caldwell 1-0 on August 16 in "the greatest game of the year," and "the prettiest game of baseball ever played on the home grounds." An error and a wild throw in the last of the ninth was the difference for Caldwell. Nampa played errorless ball — a rarity in those days. Nampa, after losing the opening games mentioned above, went on to win seven in a row and the Trolley League championship. Murphey's Cigar Store was one game back.

In August, 1914, war broke out among the great powers in Europe. It would be called the Great War because for the first time in human history the entire world would be drawn in and the lives of people and nations would be affected for the rest of the century. It began in Serbia with the assassination of an Austrian archduke, heir apparent to the throne of Austria-Hungary. The nationalist passion of Serbia helped precipitate a war that nobody wanted but that nobody could prevent. As this is written, nearly 80 years later, the Balkan conflicts of 1914 are yet to be resolved.

On August 9, 1914, war news had begun to dominate the front pages of American newspapers, but baseball, our national game, continued as before. The *Idaho Statesman* on that day headed a story about a Trolley League game, "Ball Teams Will Forget Wars Today." Few had any idea that all of American life, including baseball, would be drastically affected by events that seemed so far away.

The Idaho-Oregon League

In May, 1915, a four-team Idaho-Oregon League season got underway, with Boise, Caldwell, Nampa and Ontario as members. Ontario was expected to win, but finished second to a strong Caldwell team. Boise was last, but saw the development of some fine young players. Jack Wyman pitched both games of a double-header on May 31, 1915, and held powerful Ontario to three runs in the first game and one in the second. He struck out 17 for the afternoon. "A floating drop was the puzzler and made a lot of trouble for the batsmen who failed consistently to solve the break." All-around athlete Ollie Crites from Emmett played utility for Boise. Boise's other pitcher was Big Bill Kuss. His speed was overpowering, but his control was "hog wild," according to the *Statesman*. He walked 10 men on May 30 in a loss to Ontario. Bill Gove, veteran baseball player, team organizer and umpire of Twilight League games, managed Boise in 1915. Although the season was scheduled to run until September 1, the league folded on July 16 when Ontario and Boise quit. Poor attendance in Boise was blamed. "Conditions in this section have not been conducive to successful baseball this year," concluded the league president in his farewell statement.

Boise fans had a long wait for the last baseball game of the season. Touring big-league All-Star teams representing the American and National Leagues came through Idaho in November, 1915, playing exhibitions in any town that would pay to see them. The crowd at Twin Falls on November 9 was "immense," but very small at Shoshone next day. Both of these "exhibitions" ended in 4-4 ties, but local people who followed baseball in the newspapers cheered wildly as each well-known star was introduced.

In Boise on November 11, 1915, "The day was far too cold for a great amount of enthusiasm from either the crowd or the players." Johnny Evers, Boston Braves star, drew the biggest applause of the day when introduced. As a member of the noted Tinker-to-Evers-to-Chance double-play combination for the Chicago Cubs for many years, Evers was already a legend, and would be elected to the Hall of Fame.

The sleight-of-hand of a pepper game delighted the crowd. Four National Leaguers "had everybody guessing where the ball was going. Back of them, over their shoulders, left and right, they tossed the ball from one to another, yet each was always on the alert, and while few spectators could follow the course of the sphere, the number of misses was surprisingly small." This once popular part of the warmup before every ball game is now banned in the major leagues, and seldom seen, even in the minors. Shadow ball was another warmup display that the crowd loved. Infielders went through all the motions of scooping up grounders and throwing around the bases without a ball. The action was so convincing that the invisible ball was as real as any mime of today could make it.

When American and National League All-Star teams visited Idaho in November, 1915, it was really too cold for baseball. This photo was taken at Twin Falls.

51

The War Years

The Great War curtailed baseball activity everywhere, even before America's entry in the spring of 1917. Woodrow Wilson was reelected President in 1916 on the slogan "He kept us out of war," but the German U-Boat sinking of American ships and effective allied propaganda about German atrocities drew the country into it against Wilson's will. Thousands of the nation's best young athletes were drafted. Many volunteered even before we were at war.

Boise baseball was limited to a twilight league in 1916. Mayor Samuel H. Hayes, who had pitched in that league in his younger days, fired the first ball in opening ceremonies July 10. His catcher was Governor Moses Alexander, and the honorary batter was 69-year-old former Governor James H. Hawley.

Boise High School claimed its fourth state championship in a row, after winning nine and losing two. In addition to nearby high schools, the team beat Whitman College and Idaho Technical Institute (later Idaho State).

Although southwest Idaho had no league ball in 1916, southeast Idaho did. The Snake River-Yellowstone League fielded teams from Ashton, Driggs, Drummond, Rexburg, Rigby, St. Anthony, Sugar City and Teton City.

In 1917, the Northwest League suspended operations due to the war on July 15. All of the teams were losing money, and many of the players were about to be drafted into the service. The National Association of Professional Baseball Leagues ruled that any minor league team forced to quit because of the war had the right to "reserve its players, franchise, and territory." Most ball games played in Boise in 1917 and 1918 were between service teams and what was left of Twilight League teams. On July 1, 1917, Second Idaho Infantry Sergeant Goodwin "made baseball history," according to the *Statesman,* when, with a runner on first, he dropped a bunt two feet from home plate and stretched it into a home run. It certainly couldn't have been scored a homer, even under 1917 rules, since an error was responsible for the unusual play. The first baseman charged the ball, but the catcher got there ahead of him and fired the ball toward first, where the second baseman should have covered. He didn't, the ball rolled all the way to the tall grass in right field, and both runs scored when the relay was late.

Postwar Revival   Boise Valley could hardly wait for the 1919 baseball season to get started. Here and across the nation a golden age of sport was about to begin, only temporarily besmirched by the Chicago "Black Sox" scandal of 1919, when eight players on the American League champion White Sox team were suspended for life for conspiring to throw the World Series.

On February 8, 1919, the *Statesman* reported that many of the boys overseas had written home that they looked forward to playing organized baseball in the summer. "Six Live Southwestern Communities Ready" said the headline. Besides Boise, Caldwell, Nampa, Emmett, Wilder and Barber were said to be making plans for a new league. In the result, southwest Idaho towns organized semi-pro teams and played each other without a formal league set-up. Burley was conceded to be the state champion after it won the Southern Idaho League crown over Buhl, Filer, Twin Falls, Rupert and Paul, and beat the best town teams from the southeast and Boise Valley.

Jack Wyman, Dutch Sherman, Harry Chapman, and Mace Chapman played well for Boise in 1919, with Wyman pitching most of the games. Ernie Wells was Boise's other starter that season and pitched a two-hitter against Caldwell on Labor Day to end the season. Caldwell's star player was Anson Cornell, who as coach at the College of Idaho from 1915 until 1933, amassed record numbers of victories in every sport the college played.

The financial condition of semi-professional baseball teams in the early Twenties is wittily set forth in a letter to a stockholder in the Pocatello Baseball Association in the Snake River-Yellowstone League. The Pocatello Auto Co. had requested a certificate for the five shares in the team it had purchased sometime earlier. The league president's letter included the certificate and a comic description of its beauty and every detail: ". . . the inscription Non-Assessable . . . that, in a way, seems to make the Organization sound strong and powerful, or possibly some similar meaning, which gives the stockholder a feeling of safety. At least we found this a powerful agency in helping the sale of stock." The president then listed the assets of the Corporation, no doubt intended to make the stockholder feel that he had invested wisely:

> "One Water Bucket
> One Tin Drinking Cup
> Eight Used Baseballs (two slightly used, balance poor)
> One Pair shin guards
> Two Belly protectors
> Eleven Ball suits (differential out of two)
> Five Bats, four broken
> One hundred knockers (names withheld)"

He then added, "I will say that it was just [such] good firms as yours that really did put over the first year of professional baseball in the history of Pocatello, and we thank you."

Pocatello's American Legion team came to Caldwell in August, 1920, with a remarkable record of 41-7, best in the state. A large crowd from Boise went over to see the game. Berg, a star at the University of Oregon, pitched for Caldwell, and Boise second baseman Dutch Sherman filled in for Anse Cornell who had gone to Portland. Sam Benedict, manager of the Boise Senators in the 1930s, played third for Caldwell. Berg pitched four-hit ball and Benedict "the Caldwell right-handed Babe Ruth" brought the crowd to its feet with a long home run over the center field fence. Caldwell won 6-2. In the final game of the 1920 season Boise beat Caldwell 8-6 in a slugfest before 1,000 people.

Bill Gove managed Boise's Capitals in the Big-Four League of 1921, that included Nampa, Caldwell and Ontario. Boise won the third game of a best-of-five series from Caldwell on August 28 when Caldwell's regular catcher Sam Webb, a deputy sheriff, was unable to play because of a jail break. In September Boise won a series with Twin Falls.

That good players went to the town that made the best offer is clearly shown in the box scores for 1922. Jack Wyman still pitched good ball for Boise, backed by Jack Aschenfelter, also a fine pitcher, at third base, but the team's star second baseman Dutch Sherman played for Caldwell that year. Called "a bone of contention" for switching teams, Dutch made two errors at second base in a 17-2 April loss to Boise. One of Caldwell's runs came on a home run by "diminutive shortstop" Anse Cornell.

The Western Idaho League

Boise's entry in the Western Idaho League of 1922 got its name after Manager E.G. Rosenheim held a contest to choose one. Mountaineers was chosen over Capitols, Capitals, Governors and Senators. Mrs. Rosenheim vetoed "Rosie's Rookies." Jack Wyman had a chance to clinch the league championship in a July 21 game with Caldwell, but lost when his team committed 10 errors in an ugly exhibition of fielding. Boise did win the pennant at the end of the month and finished 12 and 3. Caldwell was three games back. In August the Mountaineers won a series with the eastern Oregon champion Baker Colts to claim the regional championship. Boise's pitching Jacks, Aschenfelter and Wyman led the team. Aschenfelter, a spitball artist, was among 14 athletes who signed up for the 1923 season in April. Al Wells was named manager, and veterans Dutch Sherman, Phil Nadeau, and Roy Johnston were back from the 1922 championship team. "Whisperin' Phil" Nadeau, who claimed to have played "several years in the majors," left the team in mid-July. Calling him "a grizzled veteran," the *Statesman* said the absence of one of the team's most reliable stickmen" was sure to hurt Boise's chances. (Nadeau, incidentally, does not appear in any major league records. Probably nobody ever checked a player's claims in those days if he could play decent ball.) The Emmett Lumberjacks won the 1923 crown. The Mountaineers finished fourth, but only two games back.

In July, 1925, Caldwell's Magicians played for what was called the "semi-professional championship of three states." LaGrande, champions of the Blue Mountain League, made up of Oregon and Washington teams east of the Cascades, came to Caldwell for a three game series that Caldwell won. Edwin "Josh" Lowell, all-time College of Idaho great, and his brother Doug, played for Caldwell. Peter Kim, young Hawaiian second baseman, also from the college, played flawless baseball and figured in two rally-ending double plays in the series. Jim Lyke at third base was also errorless in 18 chances, and got a hit in each game, two of them doubles. Josh Lowell had a home run.

The Mission Revival was in full swing when architect Fritz Hummel designed this handsome gateway to Boise's Public School Field.

1925 was the year that Cody Park passed into history. The *Idaho Statesman* waxed nostalgic over what the old park had meant to the city. "The old days at Cody Park undoubtedly will linger long in the minds of many, for in its broad expanse much of the athletic history of the state has transpired. There have been diamond battles: hard fought struggles between clubs of the Pacific Coast league, between members of the old Union Association and of the Idaho-Oregon league. And there also the local scholastic baseball championship has been threshed out for years."

Public School Field was the new name of the much improved facility south of present day East Junior High School on Warm Springs Avenue. A splendid Mission style gateway, designed by architect Fritz Hummel, framed the entry to the new field.

The Utah-Idaho League

In a meeting in Pocatello's new Bannock Hotel, March 13, 1926, the Utah-Idaho League was organized. Founding members of the Class C circuit were the Pocatello Bannocks, Salt Lake City Bees, Idaho Falls Spuds, Twin Falls Irrigators, Ogden Gunners, and Logan Collegians. This forerunner of the 1939 Pioneer League would not take in Boise as a member until 1928.

Meanwhile the Boise Mountaineers, managed by Bill Gove, continued to play in the Southern Idaho League with Caldwell, Nampa and Emmett. Boise beat Caldwell two games in the beautiful new Public School Field in the championship series at the end of August. Caldwell had won the opener 4-3, even though Sam Benedict, their former captain, hit a home run for Boise. Jim Lyke played first base for the Cockerels in the first two games and caught in the third. Boise's Jack Ashenfelter allowed but one run in the second game and pitched a shutout in the third and deciding one.

The 1926 season ended with a three game series between the Mountaineers and an All-Star team from the Utah Copper League. Boise won the first, but the visitors took the final two and went home happy.

Although the name was changed yet again, to Southwest Idaho League, the 1927 circuit was essentially the same as in 1926. Boise's Mountaineers took the title for the second season in a row. Jack Ashenfelter was the pitching standby, and such familiar names as Dutch Sherman, Sam Benedict, Ernie Wells and Roy Johnson continued to make the news.

When Boise joined the Utah-Idaho League for the 1928 season, it was with an entirely new cast of characters. Ray McKaig bought the Salt Lake City franchise in February and with it the services of 12 players. Salt Lake owner George Relf was willing to sell because Bonneville Park, longtime home of the Utah city's baseball teams had been sold for a real estate development and was going to be demolished.

Harry O'Neill, veteran pitcher, was signed to manage the team, now renamed Boise Senators. Most of his players were from southern California. League rules specified that only 14 players could be carried by a team, and on May 15, 1928, the *Idaho Statesman* ran a photograph and brief biography of the likely 14 to play for the city in the coming season. None were from Idaho. The Los Angeles Angels had options on three of the young players they had scouted during winter ball in California. Boise

Senators from 1928 who went on to the big leagues were Parke Coleman, who played for the Philadelphia Athletics and St. Louis Browns, and pitcher Leif Erickson, who had two seasons with Pittsburgh. The Utah-Idaho League class of 1928 was headed by Dolph Camilli, voted Most Valuable Player in the National League in 1941 while with Brooklyn. Lefty Gomez pitched for that same 1928 Salt Lake Bees team, and made the Hall of Fame after a great career with the New York Yankees. In 13 seasons with the team he was an All-Star seven times. In five World Series he won six games and lost none. Thornton Lee, who also pitched for the Bees in 1928, spent 15 years in the American League, four with Cleveland and 11 with the White Sox. Johnny Vergez, Ogden's 1928 shortstop, was the New York Giant's third baseman for four seasons, and finished six years in the majors with Philadelphia and St. Louis.

Boise won the first half of the 1928 Utah-Idaho League season and the powerful Salt Lake Bees won the second half going away. This set the stage for what was bally-hooed as the "Little World Series" — a best of seven like the real World Series. The plan was to play the first three games in Boise at Public School Field, and then to decide whether to finish there or go to Salt Lake for the balance of the series. President McKaig of the Senators said it would depend on fan support whether the clubs would finish in Boise or not, and that he was taking a big financial gamble.

Boise won the first game 7-3 behind the relief pitching of Manager O'Neill, a Canadian who had appeared in four games with Connie Mack's Philadelphia Athletics in 1922 and 1923. Leif Erickson, Boise's starter, gave up a leadoff home run in the first, followed by a single and three walks, the last forcing in Salt Lake's second run before O'Neill put himself in with the bases still full and only one out. He retired the next two batters and went on to pitch the remaining 8-2/3 innings, allowing one run and scattering eight hits.

Erickson began the second game, but had to be relieved by O'Neill again in the fifth inning after he had given up six runs on six hits and two bases on balls. Boise could only manage three runs, but Salt Lake hitters had a field day. Dolph Camilli hit two home runs and a single. The final score was 11-3. Next day was worse. Bees batters pounded Senator pitching for 17 hits and 14 runs. Camilli got another homer in the fourth game, won by Salt Lake 6-3, and finally on September 10, 1928, it was mercifully all over. Manager O'Neill, having nobody else to sacrifice to the

Bees' power, pitched nine innings and lost 10-2. Two Salt Lakers homered in a sad end to Boise's season, and what turned out to be the Utah-Idaho League's last game. Adding to the grief, crowds had been small and McKaig lost his shirt.

The Idaho-Intermountain League

An amateur team represented Boise in 1929. The unhappy finish of the 1928 season had killed professional ball in all of Idaho for another decade. Middleton, Emmett, Payette, Nampa and Franklin rounded out the six team league that year. Worthy of note is Payette pitcher Burt Woodward's no-hit game against Boise on the Fourth of July, 1929. His teammates committed 7 errors, but he won 9-1 anyway.

The Idaho-Eastern Oregon League

It was back to the semi-professional game again in 1930, first full year of the Great Depression. The Boise Mountaineers fielded a veteran team of former Idaho-Oregon and Western Idaho leaguers, including Jack Ashenfelter, Sam Benedict, Dutch Sherman, Ernie Wells and Manager Bill Gove. Young catcher Johnny Rasor's name appeared in the box scores for the first time that season, and he would be active for most of the decade.

Boise and Nampa played a three game set at the end of August, 1930, to decide the league championship. The Nampa Railroaders won 3-2 at home on August 17, despite a Sam Benedict home run. The second game in Boise was eked out by the Mountaineers 6-5. McIvor, Nampa's winning pitcher in the first game, pitched again with two day's rest, getting three hits himself, but lost a close one anyway. By the flip of a coin, the third and deciding game went back to Nampa. For the third time in the series, each team started its best pitcher, McIvor for Nampa, and Cecil Duff for Boise. Both were less than effective, but the Mountaineers won 9-4 on 15 hits, one of them a triple by slugger Sam Benedict.

With the Idaho-Eastern Oregon League title under their belts, the Boiseans challenged Declo, champions of the south central part of the state. Little Declo lost the first to Boise's durable Cecil Duff, but came from behind to pound the Mountaineers 11-10 in the second. Again it was Duff who held Declo to two runs and an 8-2 victory in the deciding tilt.

Called Idaho-Oregon League for the rest of the Thirties, this semi-pro circuit flourished, despite the national depression. Times were bad, but ball players wanted to play and people wanted to see the national game. Town pride, always a factor in southwest Idaho, made small burgs that had competed for years against big town Boise, want to continue. History had shown, after all, that even places as small as Declo and Emmett could compete in semi-professional baseball. They only needed two or three paid athletes, one of them a strong pitcher, to hold their own. With games scheduled for weekends, a team could get by with only one pitcher all season, if he was effective.

In April, 1932, the *Statesman* hailed a great revival of enthusiasm for the game. No less than five baseball leagues were formed in Boise that spring. The Idaho-Oregon semi-pro team began practice in Public School Field on April 13, and four other leagues held organizational meetings: the senior amateur Idaho Intermountain League; the amateur Boise Valley League; the Boise Twilight League, and the Boise and the Boise Church League.

Nyssa ventured into the Idaho-Oregon League in 1932 and played well, but was forced to drop out after the first half of a split season, won by Ontario. Leagues with uneven numbers have always had scheduling problems, but the second half of the 1932 Idaho-Oregon season continued with the Boise Senators, Nampa A.O.U.W. (Ancient Order of United Workmen), Caldwell Cockerels, Ontario Webfooters, and Emmett Loggers.

Although the United Press reported out of Chicago on July 26 that five minor leagues had already been forced to disband due to the Depression, and that several others were reduced in size, the *Statesman* countered hopefully, if ungrammatically, "Depression Don't Depress Baseball." This referred to local fan interest, and to the opportunities for seeing a wide variety of ball games. Gilkerson's Colored Giants and the Kansas City Bloomer Girls hit the valley in August for exhibition games of the kind that usually drew paying crowds. A 19-year-old pitcher named Page played for the Colored Giants against the Nampa Expressman and won a six inning exhibition 11-3 — but it couldn't have been Satchell Paige. He would have been 26 in 1932, and spelled his name with an "i". Caldwell had no trouble routing the Bloomer Girls 11-4, even though the "girls" team had four men players. The *Idaho Free Press* thought the girls played better than their male teammates, who committed a lot of errors.

Boise won the second half Idaho-Oregon League title, and took the season championship in a playoff with Ontario. They then went on a 10-day "barnstorming tour" of the Northwest. They lost at Portland, and at Kelso, Washington, but returned satisfied that they had spread the name of Boise baseball. Payette, meanwhile, won the Idaho-Intermountain League title over Wilder, Parma and Boise, which finished last.

The Idaho Penitentiary Outlaws were sponsored by the *Idaho Statesman* in 1933 and played a 17-game schedule against amateur nines from around the valley. They finished their season by taking on the semi-pro Boise Senators. Some of the convicts on the Outlaws preferred to play under assumed names, such as "Soapy Smith," "Diamond Dick," and "Al Capone."

The Idaho-Oregon League expanded from six teams in 1933 to eight in 1934. Middleton and Parma entered a league made up of Boise, Caldwell, Emmett, Nampa, Nyssa and Ontario. The Boise team, once again dubbed Mountaineers, took the first half title, but finished third in the second. In a playoff for the championship Boise beat Emmett's Loggers. Johnny Rasor was Boise's leading home run hitter in 1934. He hit two against Caldwell on July 24 and a grand slam in the last of the ninth to tie the score against the Emmett Loggers on August 5. The Mountaineers lost both games anyway, 11-9 and 13-9 when Boise's pitching just couldn't stop the opposition. Nevertheless, it was a championship season.

The 1935 Caldwell Greys.

The 1935 Idaho-Oregon League began with eight teams, but by July 1 was back to six. Playing only Sunday games, as in the past, the popular semi-pro circuit continued to draw loyal support for its teams. The Emmett Loggers won the first half title, and Boise edged out Payette for second half honors. Bill Nishioka led Emmett to a two-game sweep of the Mountaineers 5-1 and 5-4, to win the 1935 championship.

The Idaho-Intermountain League fielded eight teams in 1935. Nampa was represented by the all-Japanese Rising Suns. Some very small valley towns played that year: Melba, Bowmont, Huston, New Plymouth and Meridian, along with teams from Emmett, Caldwell and Nampa. New Plymouth beat Meridian, a town of only about 1,000 people then, to win the second half title and the chance to meet Caldwell for the championship. The Caldwell Greys won two of three and the crown for 1935 in September.

In 1936 the Rising Suns moved to Middleton and added non-Japanese players to the team. Nampa formed another nine and Bowmont, a small community south of Nampa, had no team that year. Other interesting team names in 1936 were the Meridian Buttermakers, Emmett Yearlings and Nampa Ponies. Caldwell's Greys won the first half of the split season but lost the playoffs to Meridian.

Boise's 1936 Senators were strengthened by the addition of Billy Nishioka, former Rising Sun, who had also played for Emmett's 1935 champs. The all-around ability of this noted athlete of his era is highlighted in a *Statesman* account of an August 30, 1936, playoff tilt with Payette for the league championship: "Star of the game was Nishioka, Japanese second sacker for Boise, who covered the infield and half the outfield. He was here and everywhere during the game, reached first base four times on five times at bat, made no miscues, and brought the crowd to its feet with a sensational running catch of a hard fly beyond second base, with two out and the bases full." Payette won "the south Idaho baseball championship" when its all-stars beat Boise three games to two. Emotions were high for the fifth and deciding game. Hobbs, Boise shortstop, was removed from the field by police when he struck Payette catcher Jim Lyke in the face after a collision at home plate. Boise manager Bill Gove's lineup included, in addition to Nishioka, some other local stars of the Thirties: Johnny Rasor and John Urlezaga, both catcher-outfielders; John Phillippi and veteran player-manager Sam Benedict, outfield and utility, and Noug Worthen and Roy Johnson, infield.

Johnson was business manager for Boise in the 1937 Idaho-Oregon League. When he showed off the team's new uniforms that spring, white trimmed in red, with the word "Boise" across the front in script, he said the team had not, and would not, adopt a nickname for the season. The "no-name" Boiseans of 1937 had all of the familiar names from 1936 back, however, plus a new pitcher who would lead the league and make the Boise Pilots in 1939 as a professional. His name was Larry Rene, a 25-year-old from South Dakota, who had already pitched several seasons of semi-pro ball in the upper Midwest. Boise won the championship in a playoff with Payette. Sam Benedict managed and former manager Bill Gove was elected president of the league.

The Basque duo of Johnny Urlezaga and John Anduiza gave power to Boise's lineup in 1937. Urlezaga, who could catch or play outfield as needed, grew up in Jordan Valley. His nicknames, "Dynamite," "Wildhorse" and "Battering Basque" reflect his colorful style and hitting strength. He was consistently the team leader in average and slugging percentage. He and Anduiza played for Ontario in 1938 and batted that team to the second-half title and a playoff with their former teammates at Boise — a series they won for the championship of the Idaho-Oregon League.

Boise's 1937 Senators. Standing: Larry Kinser, Manager Sam Benedict, Lingel, George Moore, Johnny Rasor, Larry Rene. Kneeling: Johnny Urlezaga, Noug Worthen, Johnny Phillippi, Billy Nishioka, Roy Johnson.

Ethnic Teams

Ethnic teams were a part of the Boise baseball scene from as early as 1905 when hardware dealer and longtime baseball supporter Jim Lusk organized an all-black team of local men to play a Fourth of July game at Riverside Park. Using the stereotypical humor of the day, the *Statesman* said "every colored player from Jim Lusk down will be searched on entering the grounds for hidden razors." (Lusk was white.) The game was described as "a very entertaining and laughable exhibition of the national game" in which "the colored team played good ball throughout."

In 1908 Boise heard about a Nez Perce Indian team from Lapwai that claimed the championship of North Idaho. In those days it was common for successful regional teams to proclaim themselves champions, and there were occasional playoffs to decide the unofficial championship of Idaho, but such arrangements were spur-of-the-moment and rarely formalized.

There is no record that Lapwai's Nez Perce of 1908 ever got to play for the state championship, but in 1925 another Lapwai squad came to Boise and beat the heavily favored Mountaineers 11 to 10. White, the Indian catcher, had three hits including a home run and a triple. The Lapwai team lost two of three that summer to Caldwell, semi-professional champions of Idaho, Oregon and Washington, through a series of playoffs. In 1936 an Umatilla Indian nine accepted a challenge from Payette's town team, but lost 18 to 8.

Japanese-American teams from Boise Valley and Eastern Oregon were prominent in the 1930s. Nampa had a team called Asahi (Rising Suns) in 1932 that played pickup games with whomever they could schedule. In August, 1932, a team made of R. Hashitani, Nishioka, Natsumura, Masuda, Matsumoto, G. Hashitani, Akithika, Fujehira and Miyake, played the Idaho State Penitentiary "Outlaws" at Outlaw Field. The Outlaws

*Three Rising Suns —
Asahi in Japanese.*

played many other local teams through the years and were sometimes allowed to travel to games outside the walls.

The Rising Suns played for Nampa in the Idaho Intermountain League starting with the 1934 season. They later represented Middleton in the same league, although in later years the team had several players who weren't Japanese. The 1934 Championship game between the Suns and Meridian was protested when it was revealed that one of the umpires had bet on Meridian.

The Tokyo Giants, Japan's big league professional champions, barnstormed the Western states in 1936. They drew a crowd of 2,000 in Boise on April 29. Eijii Sawamura, 19, called by the press "the Schoolboy Rowe" of Japanese baseball, struck out 12 Idaho All-Stars and allowed only three hits enroute to a two to one victory. He also collected two of the Giants' seven hits. "Big" McIntosh, star left-hander from Rupert, pitched a fine game for the All-Stars, striking out 10. Johnny Rasor, catcher for the Boise Senators in the Idaho-Oregon League, batted cleanup that day, got one of the All-Stars' three hits, and caught McIntosh's hard ones. Eddie Miyake of Nampa, a member of the Rising Suns team, was chosen to be one of the umpires, since none of the Japanese players spoke any English. More than 400 Japanese-Americans from Boise Valley and eastern Oregon turned out for the game, and hosted a banquet that evening in the Owyhee Hotel for the visitors from Japan.

Sawamura went on to become a baseball legend and a national hero in Japan. He died in World War II when his troopship was torpedoed by an American submarine.

"Besides being one of the finest teams ever to play here, the Tokyo Giants also have the distinction of being the most courteous," said the *Idaho Statesman*. "It is the custom of each of the Japanese players to bow and tip his hat after an umpire's decision, whether the decision is in his favor or not."

On July 5, 1936, Middleton's Rising Suns forfeited an Idaho-Intermountain League game to go to Seattle to play an exhibition against the all-Japanese Olympic Cadets of that city. The Idaho boys' win was highlighted by a grand slam home run by Matsumoto, Suns' pitcher. Bill Nishioka, who also pitched that day, was himself noted for power. On May 24, 1936, he hit "the longest home run ever hit at New Plymouth" in a victory over the 1935 champions, and was also the winning pitcher.

Barnstorming black ball clubs came to Idaho in the Thirties. Gilkerson's Union Colored Giants played the Nampa Expressmen of the Idaho-Oregon League in the summers of 1931 and 1932. "Davis, Giant first baseman . . . was a show all in himself. He caught the ball standing on his head, lying down, or what have you, and wound up a perfectly pleasant afternoon by smacking out two home runs, the longest ever hit on the local diamond . . . they haven't found the balls yet." The Detroit Colored Giants played the Boise Senators in August, 1933, and returned for a two game series in September, 1936. The black St. Louis Blues swept a three game series from the Senators in August of that year. Blacks were barred from major league baseball, but Idaho fans loved to see them play when they came in as barnstormers. They, like the famed House of David bearded teams of the time, put on an entertaining show and usually outclassed the locals they played.

Boise briefly had its own all-black team in 1932. The Boise Monarchs joined the Idaho-Intermountain League on May 1st and played four games before disbanding. The Monarchs obviously took their name from the famous Kansas City black team, regarded by some baseball historians as the equal of major league teams of their day for which no blacks could play.

The Broadway Clowns of New York City beat Nampa of the Idaho-Oregon League 6 to 4 in the spring of 1939. Douglas, the Clowns' pitcher struck out 11, but gave up home runs to Bedard and Thompson.

Not generally known is that Branch Rickey, president of the Brooklyn Dodgers, who began the desegregation of baseball's big leagues by hiring Jackie Robinson in 1947, briefly practiced law in Boise in 1912. His office was in the Idaho building. He had come west for his health after playing for the St. Louis Browns in 1905-06 and the New York Yankees in 1907. He returned to St. Louis in 1913 where he managed the Browns for three seasons and the Cardinals for seven before becoming a General Manager. He was elected to the Baseball Hall of Fame by the veterans' committee in 1967, five years after Jackie Robinson made it in 1962, his first year of eligibility. Robinson was the first black to make the Hall, just as he had been the first black in major league baseball, and is generally acknowledged to be one of the best players of all time.

Rising Suns in action.

Claude, Emmanuel, and Hal Buckner came to Idaho from Kansas in the early Twenties. All were fine athletes and played baseball in Boise.

*John Urlezaga and
Bill Nishioka, 1937.*

Mexico City's Aztecas came to Boise to play the Senators on August 19, 1936. The home team won 8 to 7. Of some local interest due to the area's large Basque population was the fact that the Mexican club's battery, Arrieola and Ibarra, were both of Basque descent, and that local Basque John "Dynamite" Urlezaga caught for Boise. In later years when the Pioneer and Northwest Leagues fielded Idaho teams, many Latin American players appeared in Boise. After blacks gained entry into major league baseball in 1947, black players were soon signed by Pioneer League Clubs. Hall-of-Famer Frank Robinson, Cincinnati and Baltimore star, and the Majors' first black manager, played for Ogden in 1953. John Roseboro, a 14-year big leaguer, caught for Great Falls in 1953.

Real ethnic diversity was seen at Airway Park on July 24, 1948, when owner Haydn Walker of the Boise Pilots booked the barnstorming Harlem Globetrotters black baseball team into

Airway Park for an exhibition game against the Hawaiian All-Stars from Honolulu. The Pilots were on the road, and it was a chance for the canny Walker to rent the park and, as he said, give local fans some variety. The Globetrotters featured Joe Bankhead, one of the five famous Bankhead brothers who had played for the Birmingham Black Barons. (His brother Dan played for the Brooklyn Dodgers in 1947 and 1950-51.) The Hawaiians, with players of Japanese, Chinese, Korean, Filipino and Puerto Rican ancestry, won the game 4 to 3.

Many fine black players have appeared in the Northwest League. Lewiston had Athletics' bonus babies Blue Moon Odom in 1965 and Reggie Jackson for a few games in 1966. Besides his all-time-best World Series slugging percentage (.755) that earned him the name "Mr. October," Reggie set other marks unlikely to be broken. He led the American League in errors five times and struck out 2,597 times — 600 more than Willie Stargell, next man on the list. Jackson hit 563 big league home runs, but his first professional "dinger," recalled in his autobiography, came at Lewiston. Rickey Henderson, who played for the Boise Athletics in 1976, is another almost certain Hall-of-Famer from the Northwest League.

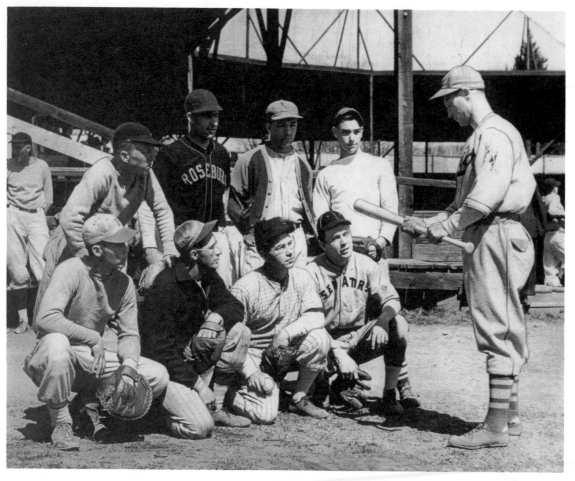

Far left: Andy Harrington conducted a baseball school for area hopefuls trying to make the new Boise Pilots team. April 4, 1939.

The Pioneer League

The Pioneer League, during the 22 years in which Boise teams were members, produced some great baseball players and a lot of very good ones. Old-timers can proudly list those who made it to the major leagues, some who had played there before, and the few elite who went all the way to the Baseball Hall of Fame at Cooperstown. They will also tell you that there were some great minor league players who could have made it with just a few breaks along the way.

Among former big-leaguers who played with Boise in those years, Andy Harrington deserves special mention. He was the Pilots' first manager when the league began operations in 1939. He hit .336 while playing second base that season, and was chosen by popular vote to manage the Western team in the league All-Star game. After the 1940 season Pilots' owner Haydn Walker sold Harrington to Twin Falls — a move received with bitterness in Boise. A newspaper editorial expressed the community's feelings:

We'll Miss Andy Harrington

Just as there was no joy in the legendary Mudville when the mighty Casey struck out, so is there regret in Boise with the announcement that Andy Harrington has been sold to Twin Falls. Harrington, in the two years that he has managed the Boise club in the Pioneer League, has done a first class job. Along with able direction of the team, he played the best second base in the league. He has been in the thick of both pennant races. He remains the most popular player in the league with the fans.

The Pioneer League is two years old. It has prospered in spite of ownership that for the most part has been more amateurish than the low paid players. Such ownership has at times undertaken to direct the management of the team while games were in actual play. This was true in Boise many times, and the fact that Harrington survived two years in such a system is a further tribute to his patience and general ability. He played the game well.

On the other hand, were it understood that the ownership of the Boise club faced financial problems, then the sale of Harrington, or any other player, would be justified. However, general opinion is that the Boise club has operated profitably. It follows then that the best reason for Harrington's sale was a few hundred dollars cash.

The new season is not far off. There likely will be many evenings this summer when Harrington will demonstrate to the owners of the Boise club what the fans already know. Andy Harrington was a part of baseball in Boise. It was a mistake to let him go.

Haydn Walker, pudgy, hard-drinking, cigar-smoking owner of the Boise Pilots, came into baseball from Spokane with a carnival background. He was all too clearly the object of the editorial criticism quoted above. Harrington was easy to like and the volatile Walker was not. He was, in many ways, the George

Andy Harrington was a Pioneer League All-Star at second base.

Owner Haydn Walker and Manager Andy Harrington check out team tryouts, April 3, 1939.

Steinbrenner of Pioneer League history. A former player remembers him as "always disgruntled" and especially disagreeable and unreasonable when he had been drinking. Unfortunately, that was often. He fired managers and players so regularly that they learned to sit tight and wait for him to cool down or sober up. He once fired the team's bus driver in the middle of Yellowstone Park. The driver got out and walked down the highway leaving the team stranded.

After a 1950 game at Great Falls, as the team was boarding the bus, he suddenly ordered Bob King, the team's young shortstop, to go back to the clubhouse and pick up all the broken bats. King, not liking Walker's tone of voice, and knowing that he had had a few drinks, replied politely, but firmly, "No, I'm not going to do that Mr. Walker," and got on the bus. Walker, apparently not sure to whom he had just spoken, walked up and down outside the bus looking in the windows for King. When he got on board and started down the aisle, Manager Ford Mullen intercepted him and said, "Those bats were all broken, Haydn, and no good to anybody." Walker fired him on the spot. Next day, in a manner that was typical after he had sobered up, he stood in front of the bus and apologized to Mullen and the team with tears in his eyes.

Andy Harrington was as popular with his team as he was with the fans. Fine players like Walt Lowe and Gordie Williamson credit him with being a great teacher of the game who did a lot for his young hopefuls. After spending the 1941 season in Twin Falls, Harrington was hired to manage the Salt Lake City Bees. He retired at the end of the 1942 season when the Pioneer League suspended operations for the duration of World War II. He had played in organized baseball for 18 seasons, successively for Detroit, Toronto, Fort Worth, New Orleans and Seattle. He played infield on championship teams at Toronto and New Orleans, and was named to the Pacific Coast League All-Star team in 1934 while with Seattle. Tired of being moved at ownership's whim, Andy bought his contract from Seattle in 1936 and managed for Yakima in the Western International League in 1937-38. As a fielder he was always among the leaders, and when he retired his lifetime batting average was .300. As a man, he batted a lot higher than that with all who knew him.

Andy Harrington, a popular manager.

Boise's contributions to the majors began with Marvin Rickert in 1939, the league's first season. The Pilots' right fielder batted .354. The husky kid from Longbranch, on Washington's Puget Sound, was called up by the Chicago Cubs in 1942. In a six-year career he played full seasons for the Cubs in 1943 and the Boston Braves in 1949, but was used sparingly in the other areas.

Gerry Staley, another Washingtonian, was born in Brush Prairie, northeast of Vancouver. He pitched two fine seasons for the Pilots, winning 22 in 1941 and 20 in 1942. His 1942 ERA of 2.72 is a club record. The durable right-hander pitched in 640 major league games over a 15-year career, the first eight with the St. Louis Cardinals where he pitched in the All-Star games of 1952 and 1953. At age 40 he was named to the 1960 American League All-Star team.

Billy Martin was known as Alfred Martin in 1946 when he played for the Idaho Falls Russets, but was already being called "Billy the Kid" by teammates, since he was, at 18, the youngest member of the squad. "Whenever we'd call him 'the Kid,'" recalled a member of the '46 team, "he'd draw like a gun fighter." Billy batted .254 in 32 games that season, and showed the scrappy disposition and will to win that characterized his big

Gordie Williamson made the 1939 Pioneer League All-Star team while with Lewiston. He later played several seasons with Boise, and managed in 1949.

73

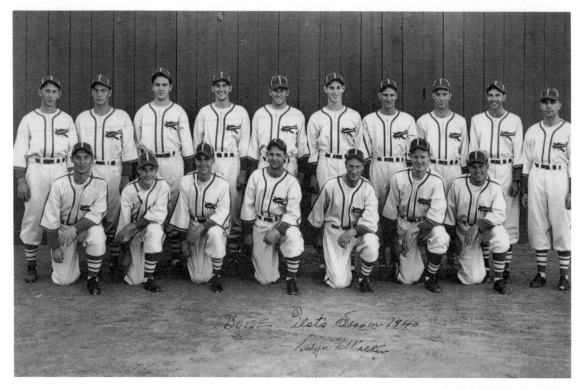

The 1940 Boise Pilots. Front row, left to right: Eddie Adams, bat boy Brewer, Gordon Williamson, Eddie Sheehan, Andy Harrington, Walt Lowe, Pop Lorenzen. Back row: Joe Egnatic, Larry Susee, Al Jaworski, Ray Bauer, Bob Price, Bob Snyder, Darrell Fields, Con Rasmussen, Jack Mentz, and Larry Rene.

league years as a player, and as manager of the New York Yankees, Minnesota Twins, Detroit Tigers, Texas Rangers and Oakland Athletics. He played 11 years in the majors, and managed for 16. He was chosen to play on the American League All-Star team in 1956, and managed his teams to five divisional pennants, two league championships, and the 1977 World Championship with the New York Yankees.

The 1948 Twin Falls Cowboys sent up Gil McDougald and Gus Triandos. McDougald was American League Rookie of the Year in 1951, and had a 10-year career with the Yankees. He was an All-Star selection five times. Triandos was in the majors 13 years and was an All-Star three times.

The 1953 Pioneer League standouts were topped by Frank Robinson who hit .348 for Ogden. His 586 home runs place him fourth on the all-time list, behind Aaron, Ruth, and Mays. (Idaho's Harmon Killebrew is fifth with 573.) Robinson began a fabulous 21-year career in the majors with Cincinnati in 1956, was American League Rookie of the Year, and voted to the All-

Star team for the first of 11 times. In 1966 with Baltimore he led the league in homers with 49; with runs-batted-in, 122; runs scored, 122; batting average, .316; on-base percentage, .415; and a slugging percentage of .637. Not surprisingly, he was voted Most Valuable Player in the American League. He had been chosen National League MVP in 1961 when he led the Cincinnati Reds to the pennant with a league-best slugging percentage of .611 and a .323 batting average. In 1982, his first year of eligibility, Robinson was elected to the Hall of Fame with a record 370 votes. In 1976 he became the first black manager in major league history. He led Cleveland three seasons, two of them as playing manager, San Francisco five seasons, and Baltimore until his retirement in 1991.

Johnny Roseboro caught for the Great Falls Electrics in 1953 and batted .310. He played 11 seasons with the Brooklyn and Los Angeles Dodgers, and was chosen to the All-Star team four times, the last in 1969 at Minnesota when he was 36, nearing the close of a 14-year career.

Bob Uecker, who has made a name as a television personality, played for the Boise Braves in 1956 and 1958. He was a lot better than his later TV persona would lead you to believe, but he was always something of a comedian. He was the team's life-of-the-party in 1956, and put up the numbers to move up the baseball ladder with 13 home runs and a .312 average in 53 games. The Braves hit for average and with power that year, and won the championship with a record 74-58. They led the league in both

Perennial Pioneer League All-Star first baseman Walter Lowe.

Andy Harrington managed the Salt Lake Bees in 1942, and again made the Pioneer League South All-Stars. Andy is second from left, front row.

The 1956 Boise Braves. Bobby King is third from left, middle row, Bob Uecker, fifth. Manager George McQuinn stands, far right.

hitting and fielding. Six Braves pitchers had winning records and five batters hit over .300. Pitcher Paul Sereduk set an all-time record by appearing in 56 games. He batted .306 and was even used as a pinch-hitter occasionally. Bob King led all shortstops in fielding, and filled in as manager from June 25 until July 1. He was also the league's best defensive shortstop in 1950, 1955, 1957 and 1958. Today he is West Coast Scouting Supervisor for the Houston Astros.

Bob Uecker was back in 1958 and did even better than in '56. He hit .322 with 21 homers and 19 doubles. Jim Kaat led the league in pitching with a record of 16-9 and an ERA of 2.99 at Missoula that year. In 1959 he was called up by the Washington Senators, moved to Minnesota with the team in 1961, and was the mainstay of the Twins pitching staff until mid-1973. He led the American League in 1966 in victories, 25; complete games, 19; and innings pitched, 304. He was selected for three All-Star games in a career that spanned an impressive 25 seasons in the majors.

Boise pitcher Paul Sereduk set a league record with 56 appearances for the 1956 league champion Braves.

Tony Cloninger pitched for the Boise Braves in 1959. He won 8 and lost 6 — not outstanding, but good enough to get him advanced to Milwaukee in 1961. He retired after a dozen seasons in 1972, with a won-lost record of 113-97. His best season was 1965 when he won 24 games, second in the league to Sandy Koufax's 26.

In 1962 Santos "Sandy" Alomar helped Boise win the season's first half pennant. The slick-fielding Puerto Rican infielder led the team in hitting with a .329 average. In 1964 he was playing for the parent Milwaukee Braves and starting a 15-season major league career. He made the American League All-Star team while playing for the California Angels in 1970, and began a baseball dynasty by being the first All-Star to have two sons also reach that level of achievement — Sandy, Jr., and Roberto, who each made the All-Star games of 1990, 1991 and 1992. In 1990 the two opposed each other. Roberto of the San Diego Padres played second base for the National League, and Sandy, Jr., of the Cleveland Indians, caught for the American League. Roberto, who made it again with Toronto in 1993 has played on two World Champion Bluejays teams.

Glen Clark, who hit 30 home runs, had 110 runs batted in and averaged .323 for Boise in 1963, played in four games for Atlanta in 1967. He was hitless in four at bats — a good example of a promising player getting "a cup of coffee" in the majors and no further chances.

The 1941 Boise Pilots.

Jim Keesey, replacement for Harrington in 1941 as Pilots manager, was another experienced veteran. He had played in a total of 16 games for Connie Mack's Philadelphia Athletics in 1925 and 1930, but had been a player-manager for Oklahoma City in the Texas League. He hit .328 there in 1940 and made only four errors all season at first base. When Keesey played first for Boise, Walt Lowe moved to center field. The Pilots won their first championship in 1941 with a record of 81-49. In 1942 they won the second half but lost to first-half winner Pocatello four games to three in the playoffs. Boise led 2-1 going into the top of the 9th in the final game, but lost a heart-breaker 3-2 when the Cardinals rallied. When the players' share of the gate receipts for the first four games was divided by league president Jack Halliwell, the winners got $60 each, the losers, $40. How times have changed!

Frank Lamanske had pitched 3-2/3 innings for the Brooklyn Dodgers in 1935 with disastrous results (5 hits, a walk and 2 runs), but managed to stick around in the minors until coming to Boise in 1942. He set a team record with a 23-8 season and an ERA of 2.74, and helped the Pilots to the second-half championship. It was his misfortune to give up the ninth-inning runs that lost the 1942 playoffs mentioned earlier.

Ford Mullen was Haydn Walker's manager in 1950. He had played in 118 games with the Philadelphia Phillies. Walker, plagued by ill health in his last years as owner of the club, finally attracted sympathy from baseball writers who had found him hard to deal with in the past. John Mooney, writing from Pocatello, called him "the most misunderstood man in the Pioneer League," and its "stormy petrel," who nevertheless deserved credit for having been one of the courageous founders of the league back in the winter of 1938-39. Mooney recalled a league meeting in Ogden when Walker, "incensed at the 'stupidity' of the other directors, held the whole meeting in abeyance by checking out of his room at the Ben Lomond and registering in another hotel under an assumed name." On another occasion, after spending most of an hour "berating" league president Jack Halliwell, he moved to increase Halliwell's salary. "The heart bled," Mooney said, of one of the subdued Walker's last appearances at a league meeting, "for one of the old fire horses who couldn't answer the alarm any more."

Haydn Walker sold the ball club to Maury Doerr of Twin Falls on June 25, 1951. Doerr, long-time supporter of baseball in Magic Valley, owned the Twin Falls franchise for a year before fulfilling a lifelong dream of returning to his home town of Boise as owner of a professional baseball team. He announced his plans to reawaken fan interest in Boise. Unlike Walker, who had constantly second-guessed his managers, Doerr promised to hire the best man he could get and let him run the club without interference. Walker had always run an independent club, without a major league connection. Doerr, who had successfully negotiated a deal with the New York Yankees while at Twin Falls, now vowed to seek a major league connection for Boise. As it turned out, he brought the Yankee arrangement with him, and in 1952 and '53 it was the Boise Yankees. Despite the Yankee connection in those years, the club finished fifth and sixth. In 1954, back to an independent status again, the Pilots finished last.

In October, 1954, a group of Boise business leaders formed Capital City Baseball, Inc., and bought out Doerr's interest. In view of the club's recent experience, it was a courageous and public spirited effort to keep professional baseball alive in Boise "for at least another year." Officers of the corporation were Robert Randall, president; Sib Kleffner, vice president; and Robert Hammersley, secretary treasurer. Other board members were William Campbell, J.R. Field, George Korfanta, Willis Moffat, and former Mayor Wes Whillock. Critical to success for the new management was an agreement reached with the Milwaukee Braves, then a powerhouse in the National League. Milwaukee finished second, one game out, in 1956, and won the pennant in 1957 and 1958. In 1957 the Braves won a memorable World Series over the Yankees, four games to three, but lost by the same margin in 1958. Lou Burdette and Warren Spahn got all of the Braves' seven wins in the two series.

Bill Campbell officiated at ceremonies honoring Meridian native Vernon Law when the Pittsburgh Pirates came to Boise to play the Braves on June 9, 1958. Campbell has been a leader and key supporter of Boise baseball for more than 40 years.

Lou Stringer, who managed Boise in 1955, had played for six seasons in the big leagues, three with the Chicago Cubs and three with the Boston Red Sox, ending in 1950. He led the team to a league championship in his only season as manager, and batted .341, but was replaced in 1956 by Mickey Livingston, a big league veteran of 10 seasons, 1938-51. Shortstop Bob King took over on June 25th until George McQuinn arrived on July 1st. Another great veteran, McQuinn had played in three All-Star games with the wartime St. Louis Browns, and was chosen for three others. He helped the Browns get to their only World Series in 1944, against the hometown St. Louis Cardinals. His two-run homer in the fourth inning of the first game gave the surprising Browns all they needed to win 2-1. The heavily favored Cardinals won the series four games to two, but McQuinn led all hitters with a .438 average. He had seven hits, including the home run and two doubles, was walked seven times, and batted in five runs. McQuinn managed the Boise Braves through the 1957 season.

Billy Smith, left, hit .390 for the Boise Braves in 1959 to top all minor league batters in America. With him at the silver bat presentation are Hall-of-Famer Harmon Killebrew, Vernon Law, Governor Robert Smylie, and Larry Jackson. Smith managed the team to three first-place finishes, 1958-60.

Billy Smith led the team from 1958 through 1960, and was followed by Gordon Maltzberger in 1961, whose Braves won the championship. Albert Unser managed in 1962 and Billy Smith came back in 1963, the team's last and worst season. Through no fault of Billy's, the Braves finished fifth, 37 games back of the champion Idaho Falls Russets.

On October 14, 1963, Sib Kleffner, president of Capital City Baseball, Inc., announced that Boise's franchise was being returned to the league. The Milwaukee Braves were notified that the team was terminating its working agreement with them. "We sincerely regret this action has to be taken," Kleffner said, "but due to lack of attendance and our present financial condition, we have no other recourse." Bill Campbell, club vice president, said that every possible way to keep professional baseball in Boise had been explored without success.

What killed baseball in Boise? The same things that would end the Pioneer League itself a year later: coverage of big league baseball on television had reduced attendance, and there was not enough support from the majors. Why drive to the ball park, pay admission to sit on uncomfortable seats for two hours or more to watch minor league talent when you could watch major league baseball from your favorite easy chair, without leaving home? And, the cold beer in your refrigerator, a few steps away, cost less than beer at the ballpark. The trips to the fridge let you stretch between innings and miss tedious commercials shown over and over. This was a national change in lifestyle that eventually shut down most of America's once-flourishing minor leagues.

Ray Giffin, veteran sports reporter for the *Idaho Statesman*, suggested this epitaph for the grand old Pioneer League: "Born 1939 and killed in a head-on collision with the major leagues, 1963." The majors had refused to give the working agreements to the minors for the 1964 season that would enable them to continue. Without major league support, most teams would lose money. Another factor that had reduced major league farm systems by 1963 was the increased importance of college baseball as the place where young players were developed. The colleges and universities supplied talented and well-coached professional material, some of it ready for the majors without years of minor league seasoning.

Boise's Pioneer League Highlights 1939-63

Boldface Indicates Played in Major Leagues
*Indicates Best in League

YEAR	MANAGER	LEADING HITTERS		LEADING FIELDERS		LEADING PITCHERS		FINISH
1939 PILOTS	**Andy Harrington**	Edw. F. Adams **Marv Rickert** **Andy Harrington** Walt Lowe	.377 .354 .336 .331	Walt Lowe, 1B, **Andy Harrington**, 2B Ed Sheehan, 3B	.987* .984* .926*	Jack Mentz Larry Rene	17-7 13-8	Third
1940 PILOTS	**Andy Harrington**	Walt Lowe (22 HR, 121 RBI*) Edw. Adams	.341 .311	**Andy Harrington**, 2B James Donovan, 3B Ed Sheehan, SS	.983* .949* .924*	Jack Mentz Con Rasmussen	15-10 14-13	Second
1941 PILOTS	**Jim Keesey**	**Jim Keesey** **John Radtke** Gordon Williamson	.323 .321 .306	**John Radtke**, 2B Walt Lowe, 1B	.966* .989*	**Gerry Staley** Bob Snyder Larry Susee	22-8 21-9 17-9	First
1942 PILOTS	**Jim Keesey**	Al Korhonen	.339	Lou Tamone, SS	.889*	**Frank Lamanske** **Gerry Staley**	23-8* 20-10	First 2nd Half
		League suspended play 1943-45 due to World War II						
1946 PILOTS	Walt Lowe	Walt Lowe (23 HR)	.318	Bill Stenger, SS	.941*	Bob Kerrigan	18-14	Fifth
1947 PILOTS	Walt Lowe	Walt Lowe (22 HR, 157 RBI*) Ed Daniels Dave Molitor	.357 .322 .316	Walt Lowe, 1B	.990*	Bill Franks Bob Roberts	20-14 13-7	Fourth
1948 PILOTS	Walt Lowe	Ed Daniels Walt Lowe	.313 .302	Ed Daniels, OF Walt Lowe, 1B	.980* .992*	Bill Franks (194 SO*) Dick Colombo	23-15 13-10	Sixth
1949 PILOTS	Bill Stenger (To July 2) Gordon Williamson	Jim O'Brien Frank Constantino	.366 .318			Dick Conover Jim Gilmore	12-10 8-6	Seventh
1950 PILOTS	**Ford Mullen**	Jim O'Brien	.3	Bobbie King, SS	.957*	Bill Franks	12-8	Seventh
1951 PILOTS	Tom Lloyd (To May 21) Frank Gregory	(No Regular Hit)	.300			(No pitcher had winning record)		Eighth

YEAR	MANAGER	LEADING HITTERS		LEADING FIELDERS		LEADING PITCHERS		FINISH
1952 YANKEES	L. Wayne Tucker	Bob Martin	.341			Frank Cirimelli	21-11	Fifth
1953 YANKEES	**Tedd Gullic**	(No Regular Hit .300)				John James Gene Carlson	14-9 11-5	Sixth
1954 PILOTS	Edward Fernandez	(No Regular Hit .300)		Ernesto Sierra, SS	.958*	Gordon Tench	6-5	Eighth
1955 BRAVES	**Louis Stringer**	Arnold Hallgren (37 2B, 19 HR, 139 RBI*) **Lou Stringer**	.348* .341	Bobbie King, SS Dick Morse, 3B	.958* .944*	John Stadniki J. Adkins James Espinola Del Coursey Paul Sereduk	7-2 7-4 15-9 10-4 6-2	First
1956 BRAVES	**Mickey Livingston** (To June 25) Bob King (To July 1) **George McQuinn**	Leonard Williams (24 HR) Rufus Johnson (10 HR) **Bob Uecker** (13 HR in 53 games)	.352 .338 .312			Robert Arendt Del Coursey Paul Sereduk Noel Mickelsen	15-7 15-8 10-7 12-7	First 74-58
1957 BRAVES	**George McQuinn**	Maurice Lerner Rufus Johnson Robert Jacoby	.328 .319 .316	Bobbie King, SS Howard Bedell, OF	.972* .970*	Robert Botz Winston Brown Roger Clapp	6-3 14-10 12-10	Fourth
1958 BRAVES	Billy Smith	**Bob Uecker** (21 HR, 19 2B) John Garafalo Billy Smith	.322 .329 .315	Billy Smith, 1B Tom Brown, 3B Bobbie King, SS	.991* .922* .964*	John Stokoe C. William Holmes Roger Clapp Clifford Jones	10-7 17-12 11-5 14-18	First, 2nd Half
1959 BRAVES	Billy Smith	Billy Smith Kerry Buckner	.390* .340	Mike Fandozzi, 1B	.990*	Leslie Bass **Tony Cloninger** David Scranton	21-3 8-6 11-8	First
1960 BRAVES	Billy Smith	Raymond Reed Roberto Barbosa Hermond Hubbard	.347 .330 .325	Clayton, 2B Lucas, 3B	.957 .977	**David Eilers** **Herb Hippauf** Roberto Barbosa	15-8 14-8 12-8	First 1st Half

YEAR	MANAGER	LEADING HITTERS		LEADING FIELDERS		LEADING PITCHERS		FINISH
1961 BRAVES	Gordon Maltzberger	**George Kopacz** Clayton Douglas	.327 .316	**George Kopacz**, 1B Clayton, 2B Powell, C	.978* .966* .984	Ryan Rich Holden Harold Gelein	13-5 10-4 9-5	First 72-55
1962 BRAVES	Albert Unser	**Santos Alomar** Marcial Allen	.329 .325			**Clay Carroll** Fred Alworth	14-7 12-6	First 1st Half
1963 BRAVES	Billy Smith	**Glenn Clark** (30 HR, 110 RBI)	.323			Eugene Garnell (Only Pitcher over .500)	9-7	Last (37 games out)

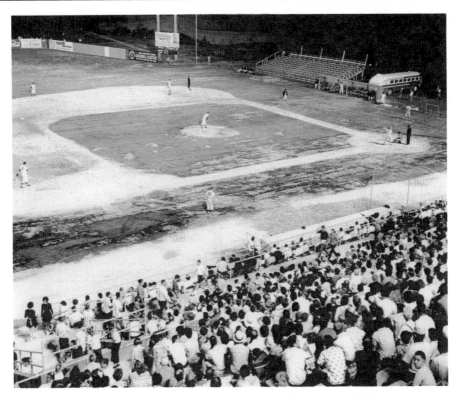

The Treasure Valley Cubs played in a new rookie league in 1964. Canyon County Multi-Purpose Stadium, across the street from The College of Idaho in Caldwell (now Simplot Stadium), is the legacy of that last gasp of professional baseball in Boise Valley for a decade.

Airway Park was the beautiful home of the Boise Pilots and Boise Braves from 1939 until 1963.

Airway Park, the superb home of Boise's Pioneer League teams for a quarter century, was built in the spring of 1939 in time for the season home opener. The Boise Park Corporation leased 9½ acres of land from the city at the intersection of Maple Street and Park Boulevard, near the river, on March 6, 1939. The price was $1500, payable over a 10-year period. Melvin C. Smith, president of the corporation, challenged the directors to raise enough money in the next 10 days to get construction started. Haydn Walker, owner-president of the Pilots, reminded directors that the park had to be ready in less than two months. On March 13, Smith announced that $5000 in cash had been raised and another $4566 pledged, and that work could begin.

Long regarded as one of the finest minor league ball parks in the country, due in no small measure to the devotion and skill of live-in groundskeeper Ed Turnbaugh, Airway Park was sold to the State of Idaho in November, 1963. The park, then called

Braves Field, was demolished to make way for the present Fish and Game Department office building. The Turnbaughs raised a family in their home under the grandstand, and Mrs. Turnbaugh ran ballpark concessions. Years later, when he met a Boisean at a charity golf tournament, Billy Martin said, "What a shame they tore down that beautiful ball park you had there in Boise."

Among the fine Boise Pioneer League players who never got called up at all, a few stand out as truly great minor leaguers. When the centennial of baseball was celebrated at Cooperstown, New York, in July, 1939, Walter Lowe of the Boise Pilots was chosen to represent the Pioneer League in a minor league All-Star game. Since there were 42 minor leagues in 1939, only one

Haydn Walker looks on as Mayor James Straight wishes Walt Lowe good luck, as the Pioneer League's representative at Cooperstown to help celebrate the 1939 Centennial of Baseball. Mel Smith was president of the Boise Park Corporation.

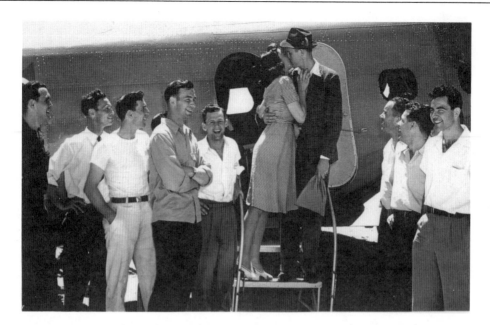

Teammates watch newlyweds Walt and Irene Lowe kiss good-bye as he heads for the All-Star game at Cooperstown. Left to right: Frank Plouf, Andy Harrington, Federmeyer, Hal Ritten, Eddie Sheehan, Con Rasmussen, Pop Lorenzen, and Jack Mentz.

player from a league was chosen. The stars were then divided into two teams for the big game played July 9. Lowe earned the right to represent his league by being an outstanding fielder at first base, by hitting .346, and by leading in homers with 23. Local fans turned out for Walter Lowe Night at Airway Park to honor their star first baseman at the last game before he left for New York. He got to play 7 innings at Cooperstown, longer than most, was errorless, made 11 putouts, and batted in a run.

Lowe was named to the Western team for the league's All-Star game that summer. Boise's Andy Harrington managed. Other Pilots who played were Ned Sheehan, infield, Marv Rickert, right field, and pitchers Jack Mentz and Con Rasmussen. The West won 4-3, despite being held to only four hits. The East made four errors, and that was the difference.

Walt Lowe led the league's first basemen in fielding in 1939 and 1947. He led in runs-batted-in in 1940 with 121, and in 1947 with 157. He was an All-Star again, and the league's Most Valuable Player in 1940 when he hit 22 homers and batted .341. His 1939 totals of 36 homers and 303 total bases are club records. After a season and a half with San Diego of the Pacific Coast League in 1943 and 1944, Walt went into the service. Upon his return he managed Boise from 1946 through 1948 and continued to play first base. His stats for those years are impressive: 1946, .318, 23

alt Lowe.

homers, 31 doubles; 1947, .357, 22 homers, 36 doubles; 1948, .302, 14 homers, 33 doubles. His fielding ranked near the top in those years as well. In 1949 he managed the Pocatello Cardinals to a third place finish, only 3½ games out of first. It's hard to believe that Walt Lowe never made the majors, but he is one of the Pioneer League's all-time greats. He maintained his connection with Boise baseball by broadcasting the team's games on radio for another 13 years until the Pioneer League folded. His sign-off, "Good night to all good sports," was familiar to a generation of fans.

Jack Halliwell, the Pioneer League's Mr. Baseball, standing outside the Pocatello ball park, named in his honor.

Mr. Baseball

Jack Halliwell of Pocatello probably had more influence on professional baseball in Idaho than any other single person. He was a founder in 1926 of the Utah-Idaho League, a class C circuit composed of Pocatello, Salt Lake City, Ogden, Logan, Idaho Falls and Twin Falls. In 1928, its last year of operation, Boise joined a reduced four-team league that included Salt Lake City, Pocatello and Ogden.

Usually regarded as the natural forerunner of the Pioneer League of 1939, the Utah-Idaho League was centered in the same intermountain area, and had the same dedicated and experienced leadership. Jack Halliwell was vice president and acting president of the Utah-Idaho League, and president of the Pioneer League for the first 14 years of its existence. He ran the show with firmness, fairness and diplomacy, winning the respect of all who came in contact with him. It was a tough job, and on his retirement at the end of the 1952 season, Halliwell told the *Salt*

Pioneer League President Jack Halliwell poses with the Pocatello Cardinals in Halliwell Park.

Lake Tribune "I worry too much. The pressure of constantly correcting players, backing up umpires and then getting in bad with everybody simply is too much for a man of my age." He was 63 at the time.

While getting a degree in pharmacy at Northwestern University, Halliwell caught for the varsity baseball team. He came to Pocatello in 1911 and went to work in a local pharmacy. His own Halliwell Drug Co. would, in later years, be one of the city's most prominent businesses. He played amateur and semi-pro baseball, including a stint with the Snake River League of the 1920s, an "outlaw league" made up of Pocatello, Rigby, Blackfoot, Idaho Falls, Rexburg and St. Anthony. It was "outlaw" because it allowed Chick Gandil and Win Noyes of the infamous Chicago "Black Sox" of 1919 to play after they had been banned for life from professional baseball for conspiring with gamblers to throw the 1919 World Series to the Cincinnati Reds. Win Noyes, who had pitched only six innings for the White Sox in 1919, and who did not appear in the tainted World Series, pitched for Pocatello.

When he died in 1966 at age 77, tributes to what he had done for baseball came from executives and former players all over the country. Few remembered or cared that among other contributions to his community he had served in the Idaho legislature and on the Pocatello city council. Jack would have agreed that his dedication to baseball overshadowed everything else.

Salt Lake City's Deseret News gave this tribute to Jack Halliwell.

The Northwest League

Lewiston represented Idaho in the Northwest League from 1955 through 1974. Boise joined in 1975. Hillis Lane, who managed Lewiston until 1959, led the league in batting in 1955 with a lofty .391 average, second all-time to Ron McNeely's .403 in 1976 in Boise. Lane's '58 team won the second half of a split season but lost in the playoff to Yakima.

Hub Kittle, who had managed Salt Lake City in the Pioneer League in 1951 and 1952, was Yakima's manager in 1958. He had won the Pioneer League championship in 1951, and as a relief pitcher in 1952 had a dandy ERA of 1.94. Between 1955 and 1959 he led Yakima to three Northwest League pennants.

John McNamara, Lewiston's catcher in 1955, set a league record with 93 assists. In 1958, his 892 putouts and 15 double plays set records that still stand. In 1959 when he took over as playing manager, his 54 consecutive games without an error tied another league record. Mac's 1961 club won the Northwest League championship. In 1969 McNamara began a long major league managerial career at Oakland. He managed San Diego, 1974-77; Cincinnati, 1979-82; California 1983-84; Boston, 1985-88; and Cleveland, 1990-91. His 1986 Red Sox won the American League flag, but lost to the New York Mets 4 games to 3 in the World Series.

Hub Kittle returned to Yakima in 1964. He took his club from last in the first half to first in the second, and won the playoff with Eugene 3 games to 0. Although he never became a big-league manager, Hub Kittle has been a pitching coach for Houston, St. Louis, and the New York Yankees.

Lewiston's 1965 season is memorable for two reasons. The club won the first half of the split season with a 46-23 record, and Hall-of-Famer Reggie Jackson began his professional career there. According to Jackson's autobiography, Athletics owner Charlie Finley took him out of Lewiston after he had been beaned in a game, because a local hospital refused him a private room, purportedly because he was black. Lewiston people deny that Jackson's race had anything to do with it, saying there was no private room available. Bill Posedell, who coached Lewiston part of that season, is reportedly the one who called Finley with the discrimination charge.

1974 was Lewiston's last season in the Northwest League, and 1975 was Boise's first. Playing at Borah High School field under rookie manager Tom Trebelhorn, the A's farm team finished last in the Southern Division, 14½ games back, despite a .500 record.

Mike Rodriguez, Boise's DH, and shortstop Woody Woodard were selected by sports writers from league cities to the 1975 All-Star team. In 1976 the A's were below .500, despite Rodriguez' league-leading home run total and Ron McNeely's dazzling .403 batting average — the only .400 season in Northwest League history. Both made the '76 All-Star team. Not chosen was future superstar Rickey Henderson, who played an outstanding center field for Boise that year, and hit .330.

Poor attendance in the 1976 season was a warning that Boise could lose professional baseball again. When Randy Green pitched a four-hit shutout over Seattle on August 28, 1976, there were only 47 people in the stands. For the entire year the team drew 1,000 people only three times — on opening night, on the third night of the season, and on August 11 when Bob Feller gave out autographed pictures and hot dogs to the kids. People were drawn to the park to see a legend, but didn't keep coming to see the young A's — some of them just out of high school. After suffering heavy financial losses, Mike Manning, president, general manager and principal owner of the A's, said he couldn't see any way to continue. "In my worst dreams I never imagined we'd draw 200 people," he said. "I thought 400 would be rock bottom in a town this size."

Because Borah Field was under control of the school board, the sale of beer at games was not allowed. This, in Manning's mind, made a critical difference between losing money or breaking even. The board rejected a compromise plan to place a beer stand far down the right field line, away from the school building.

With a 9-8 loss on the last day of the season, the A's dropped 12 games behind Walla Walla. "It was frustrating," said manager Trebelhorn. "That was the 19th game in the last 32 that we have taken the early lead and couldn't hold it." Among the few from Boise's 1976 A's who made it to the Major Leagues, manager Tom Trebelhorn is a standout. He managed the Cleveland Indians from 1986 through 1991 and now manages the Chicago Cubs. Other outstanding big-leaguers who played in the Northwest League include Ron Cey, who led the league in runs batted in in 1968 at Tri-Cities, and had a 17-year career, 12 with the Dodgers; Julio Franco, who tied for the home run lead in 1979 at Central Oregon, led all shortstops in assists, and has spent a dozen years with Philadelphia, Cleveland and Texas; and Tony Gwynn, who led the league in batting in 1981 while playing for Walla Walla, then went directly to San Diego in 1982 where in 11 seasons he has won four batting titles and played in eight all-star games. He is a sure Hall-of-Famer.

The Boise Buckskins

The Boise Buckskins of 1978 were certainly one of the most colorful and controversial teams in Idaho's baseball history. They began with a collective dream — to get the chance to play professional baseball and to be noticed by major league scouts who had overlooked them before. Some were outstanding college players who had not been drafted, like Emil Drzayich who had broken six of Hall-of-Famer Mike Schmidt's records at Ohio University, including career home runs. He hit .400 in his junior year, yet nobody signed him.

Buckskin management also had a dream — to devise a formula that would give good young players, and a few veterans another chance. It was called "self sponsorship." Players had to find a backer willing to put $3,000 into a team kitty out of which the season's expenses would be paid — including a modest pay-back in salary, about $600 per month. Most players figured to get back about half of their investment in themselves, just for the chance to play, and hopefully to be drafted by a higher league.

It began with dreams and ended, for some at least, as a nightmare. The tone for the season was set on opening night when female General Manager Lanny Moss and field manager Gerry Craft dedicated the season to Jesus Christ. In a church-going community like Boise, this did not raise any eyebrows, and may have won some friends. After all, most public meetings, sessions of the Idaho Legislature, and civic club meetings began with a Christian invocation. Non-believers were used to it, and generally accepted it as traditional at least.

"Buckskin Bill," Idaho loner from the Salmon River country, made famous by the book *Last of the Mountain Men,* was flown to Boise to throw out the first ball. Bill, whose real name was Sylvan Hart, told reporters he had not thrown a baseball since 1918 when he was a grade-schooler in Oklahoma. His fur hat, fringed buckskin shirt and pants added enough color to the inaugural Buckskin game that CBS news came to Boise to cover the event.

That first game was a big success. Danny Thomas, former Milwaukee Brewer, ripped four hits and drove in five runs to lead his team to an 11-3 victory over the Salem Senators. Alas, the Buckskins then lost the next 12 games in a row, during which the team's glaring lack of pitching strength became apparent to all. The hitters, led by Thomas and first baseman Drzayich, continued strong, but with opponents getting successively 14, 11, 10, 25 and 12 runs in the next five games, there was little chance of winning.

Emil Drzayich, Buckskins' star first baseman, 1978.

Manager Gerry Craft, a devout young Christian, made the mistake of putting the Buckskins' trials into a religious context. He was quoted in the *Statesman* on June 28 by reporter Scott Peyron as saying, "We're being tested by Jesus Christ . . . He's testing us to the max — just like He humbled Himself before being lifted up." Players questioned by Peyron insisted that the religious atmosphere in the clubhouse, including daily prayer meetings of Craft, Moss, and some of the coaches, hadn't "broken up the loose, free-spirited atmosphere that normally surrounds a baseball team." Fifteen years later, some of the players still remember it that way. "We were a bunch of young guys who wanted to play ball. The religion thing was not that big a deal at the time."

It became a big deal in the press, however, when Gerry Craft and General Manager Lanny Moss, self-proclaimed born-again Christian, agreed to fire pitcher-infielder Brad Kramer. The *Statesman* headline next day said, "Buckskins release player after advice by God." Craft was quoted as saying, "He [God] made it very clear to me that Kramer should be released," and from then on the press seized on the fact that Boise's young manager talked to God about how to run his ball club. It even made *Sports Illustrated* on July 10, 1978.

Gerry Craft, now Northeast Scouting Supervisor for the Houston Astros, realizes he made some youthful mistakes in judgment that brought the press to its focus on religion in baseball. He says, "My first big mistake was talking to Brad Kramer about religious matters when I released him. Brad was of course in a lot of pain being released, and I was under a lot of stress letting him go. Remember, I'm the guy who went through five releases in my career. Neither of us were in the state of mind to discuss religion. From there, Brad chose to go to the press."

The reasons Kramer was released were, as reported in the press at the time, that he openly criticized the play of his teammates, and told young Buckskin pitchers they were not good enough to pitch in the Northwest League. He was late for team functions and was generally destructive of team morale. But, Craft realizes today, "My greatest mistake was saying even one time 'God told me.'" Perhaps all who pray "talk to God" or ask for Divine guidance, and most believe that God answers prayer, but the phrase "God told me" was bound to be controversial.

Although undoubtedly the most memorable feature of the 1978 Buckskins season, the press coverage of the incident lasted less than two weeks, but obscured for many a 72-game season of

Playing Manager Gerry Craft.

The Boise Buckskins were a fun-loving bunch, on and off the field. From left: Duane Robbins, Rich Martin, Emil Drzayich, Mike Price, Dave Winters, Jeff McKay, Tommy Jones. Front: Terry Bass and Bo McConnaughy.

baseball that was not all bad. Considering the young men on the team were largely paying their own way, and that as an independent team there was no parent organization to send down the needed pitching talent, nor money to buy it, the 1978 Buckskins were better than many thought at the time. Were those 12 losses in a row early in the season a league record? Hardly. Bellingham lost its first 25 in a row in the Northwest League's 1975 season. Was the team's final win percentage of .319 the league's worst? Not that either. Since 1955 no less than 12 Northwest League clubs have done worse, including most recently Bend with .284 in 1986, and Spokane with .316 in 1991.

As noted earlier, the Buckskins were a good hitting team that could have won a lot more games with even average pitching. Danny Thomas, who had been named the Eastern League's Most Valuable Player in 1976, before being called up to Milwaukee for 54 games in 1976-77, led the Northwest League in hitting with an average of .358. Called "the Sundown Kid" by teammates because his religion would not allow him to play from sundown Friday to sundown Saturday, Thomas would walk off the field the minute the sun set, no matter what the game situation. Fellow players remember him as an awesome hitter, moody, and either placid or explosive from moment to moment. Gerry Craft remembers him as a man with emotional problems which led to his tragic suicide in a jail cell in Mobile, Alabama, on June 14, 1980.

To sum up the Boise Buckskins of 1978 we can characterize them best as a group of young men who shared an American dream — to be professionals in the game they loved. Asked 15 years later about the hardships, those long and aching rides in the rickety old team bus, with its makeshift bunk beds in the back, and a propensity to break down, the bad food with too small a meal allowance, the pain of losing day after day, having to raise your own salary, the negative press coverage, and the failure to be noticed by major league scouts, they all, to a man, said it was an experience they'd not trade for anything in the world. If they could turn back the clock and try it again, they'd do it in a minute. They had the dream.

The Boise Hawks

After nine long years without professional baseball, Boise fans got something to cheer about in 1987 when Diamond Sports, Inc., of New York bought the Tri-Cities franchise in the Northwest League. Tri-Cities, like the ill-fated Buckskins of 1978, was an independent club playing in a league largely made up of teams with major league affiliations: Bellingham (Seattle); Eugene (Kansas City); Everett (San Francisco); Medford (Oakland); Salem (California); and Spokane (San Diego). Bend was listed as co-op.

Bill Wigle Field at Borah High School, home of Northwest League teams in 1975-76, 1978 and 1987-88.

Diamond Sports, headed by Ed Kranepool, former New York Mets first baseman, had operated Tri-Cities in 1983 and 1984 before selling it in 1985. Mal Fichman had been the club's general manager for those two years, and had brought the Triplets from eight games back in the Washington Division in 1983 to first in 1984, and a playoff win over Oregon Division leader Medford for the championship. For this he was chosen Northwest League Executive of the Year.

When Diamond Sports sold the franchise, Fichman went to the Class A Miami Marlins of the Florida State League. He made *Sports Illustrated* in April, 1985, for his initiative in signing former big-leaguers to work for peanuts for another chance to play and the hope that they would again be picked up by a major league club. Mike Torrez and Derrel Thomas were among the veterans Fichman signed at Miami and when Diamond Sports again bought the Tri-Cities franchise in 1986, with plans to move it to Boise in 1987, Fichman was hired as general manager and Thomas as field manager. Derrel Thomas was a veteran of 15 major league seasons with San Diego, San Francisco and Los Angeles, highlighted by one Division Series, two Championship Series, and one World Series — all with the Dodgers. He had never managed before coming to Boise. Three thousand one hundred and nine fans turned out for the 1987 season opener at Bill Wigle Field, named for Borah High School's longtime baseball coach. Bill worked over many years to create a fine ballpark with student labor, donated materials and very little money. This, with many improvements, was the same field where the ill-fated Boise Northwest League teams of 1975, '76 and '78 had played.

After a 9-28 start, rookie manager Derrel Thomas was fired by General Manager Mal Fichman. "This was one of the hardest things I've had to do," said Fichman on July 26, 1987. "I hired him and he's a friend of mine. I hope he remains a friend." Thomas, one of only six black managers in the minor leagues, admitted that he couldn't relate to the players. "It was my fault completely. I can't blame the owners or management. It was bad judgment on my part."

Mal Fichman explains the ground rules of Bill Wigle Field to Spokane's manager and umpires.

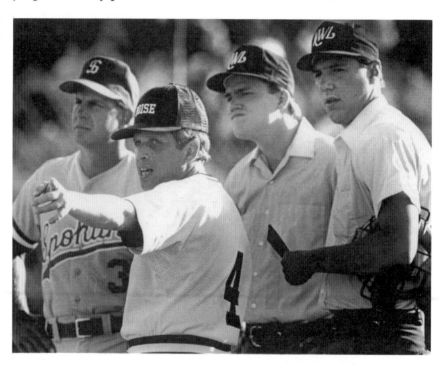

Mal Fichman took over as team manager, and continued as general manager for the rest of 1987. His aggressive style and blunt speech won him few friends in Boise. "I'm competitive," he told a reporter, "At times, I think, too competitive," and he admitted that not everybody liked his straightforward style. As the end of the 1987 season approached, Fichman told the papers,

"We may be in last place, but at least we control our own fate. If we stink, it's my fault. But if we win, it's also my fault."

The final standings showed Boise 28 games out of first place, with the worst record in the league. Fichman strongly resisted the idea of a major league affiliation, and was proud of his ability to manage a club with the smallest operating budget in the league. He released these numbers in August, and optimistically projected a break-even season: players' salaries, $101,000; front office expense, $100,000; stadium expense, including rent, ushers, ground crew, utilities and advertising, $50,000; one-time expense of renovating Bill Wigle Field, including new lights and paint, $43,000; start-up costs, including Fichman's moving expenses, $6,000. Total: $300,000.

In May, 1988, Hawks' President Ed Kranepool announced that Fichman would continue to manage the team in 1988, and credited him with "turning the club around" after taking over in July. (His record as manager in '87 was 17-22.) Boise led the league in several categories that season, but all of them negative: most games lost, most hits allowed, most runs allowed, and most home runs allowed. The Hawks were second in team batting, but a distant last in pitching, with a team ERA of 5.64. It was obvious to many old baseball hands in Boise that whatever could be said of management's handling of the team, there just weren't enough good players on the roster, and that as an independent the franchise was not likely to get them. To Fichman, independence and the ability to run the show himself was important, and he continued to resist a working connection with a major team. His 1988 team finished 12 games out with a record of 30-46. The 1989 team was second in the league's Northern Division, but with a losing record of 35-40.

In 1988 the Hawks' pattern of good hitting and weak pitching shows up glaringly in the year-end statistics. The team led the league in hitting, with best average, .274, most hits, most total bases, most doubles, fewest strikeouts, and highest slugging percentage. In pitching the staff led the league in both hits and earned runs allowed. Jeffrey Mace, a standout on both offense and defense in his two seasons with the Hawks in '87 and '88, led all outfielders in 1987 in putouts and assists while batting .340 and hitting 11 home runs. In 1988 he led the league in times at bat and total bases and on defense, led all outfielders in assists. He was edged out in fielding percentage in 1987 by a young outfielder at Bellingham named Ken Griffey, Jr.

In October, 1988, Bill Pereira, president and CEO of Diamond Sports, Inc., announced that land had been leased at the Western Idaho Fairgrounds for the construction of "one of *the* top fields in all of minor league baseball." New Hawks General Manager Fred Kuenzi added, "Our fans will be treated to a first-class operation," and said that they would no longer suffer from Wigle Field's uncomfortable wooden bleacher seats or "excruciatingly long lines to the bathroom." The new home of the Hawks was named Memorial Stadium in honor of veterans of World War II and all other armed conflicts. It was projected to cost $1.1 million.

Hall of Famer Harmon Killebrew of Payette was on hand for the beginning of the Hawks' 1989 season on June 19. Spokane, league champs in '87 and '88, spoiled the Hawks' opener in the new stadium by pounding the pitching for a 12-3 win. "I hate Opening Day," said Mal Fichman, who had now lost three of them in a row. Pessimistic *Statesman* columnist Jeff Welsch wrote, "New stadium. Old Hawks." The team made, according to manager Fichman's count, "two physical errors that led to runs . . . but a lot of mental errors. The mental mistakes cost us six runs." The official scorer charged the Hawks with three errors.

The 4,839 fans who turned out that historic night didn't like the score but they were thrilled with the new ball park. The view of the Boise foothills at dusk, the clear sky, the wall of fluttering cottonwood trees beyond the left field fence, marking the course of Boise River, made this a beautiful setting for baseball. People were pleased that the city had the finest facility since Airway Park/Braves Field was torn down 25 years earlier.

On October 11, 1989, Diamond Sports announced the signing of a player-development contract with the California Angels. "Fichman's reign comes to an end" read one headline, and "Hawks fans welcome Angels with open arms" read another. Tom Kotchman, Manager of the Year three times in his minor league career, was named by the California Angels to take over the Hawks for the 1990 season. He had managed the Angels' AAA team at Edmonton for three seasons before being sent to Boise's Class A team. He said he didn't regard it as a demotion, but as a chance to develop young talent. "You have to be able to teach, especially at this level. The players aren't as polished as they are at Triple-A. And you have to be organized." Not everyone was optimistic that the new regime would improve baseball in Boise. The ever-critical Jeff Welsch, who wrote an

Ooh, that smarts! Eugene's Les Norman slams into Hawks' second baseman Jim Sears. He was out.

opinion column for the *Statesman*, called it "A Change in Name Only," and pointed to the generally poor showing of Angels' farm teams in the Northwest league in the past. Since winning at Salem in 1982, the Bend franchise had two last place finishes, "a batting average of .232 and a bad-will mark of nearly 1.000," according to Welsch. He quoted a Bend sportswriter's open letter to the Angel's director of minor league operations. "Losing the Angels will not break the hearts of many baseball fans in Central Oregon. Your two years at Vince Genna Stadium was enough to make even longtime California fans root for your hated cross-town rivals the Dodgers." He warned that Boise fans would soon be disenchanted with the Angels if they kept sending out "some light-hitting infielder with hands of stone game after game."

In 1990, under new manager Tom Kotchman, the Angels-nourished Hawks won 53 and lost only 23 for a league-leading .697 percentage. The parent club was able to supply what the independent Hawks had long needed but never had — consistent pitching. The team ERA of 2.41 was the league's best. Hilly Hathaway, called up to the Angels in 1992, and now with the Padres, was 8-2 with a superb 1.46 ERA, and led the league with 113 strikeouts. Teammate Phil Leftwich also went 8-2 and had 1.86 ERA. He also was called up by the parent club. The Hawks lost the championship series to Northern Division winners Spokane, two games to one. It was a heartbreaking loss for the young Hawks, but it had been a great season.

The league champion Boise Hawks celebrate their playoff victory over Yakima, August 29, 1991.

Chris Turner, record-setting catcher.

In 1991 Tom Kotchman's Hawks won it all. They won 50, lost 26, and swept Yakima two straight for the championship. Julian Heredia led the league in strikeouts with 99, in ERA with 1.05, and won eight while losing only one. Catcher Chris Turner set an all-time league record with a .99748 fielding percentage, and relief pitcher Troy Percival led the league in saves with 12.

The 1992 Hawks had a winning season, 40-36, but finished second in the Southern Division to Bend. Reliever John Pricher led the league with 23 saves and had an ERA of 1.05. In 32 games he gave up only five earned runs and one homer while striking out 65. Mike Butler was the most successful starter with a 9-5 record. He topped the staff with 91 strikeouts. Chris Anderson hit .309 and topped the batters. Mickey Kerns led in runs batted in, had nine homers, four triples and 14 doubles, but struck out 99 times in 69 games.

In 1993, just 125 years after Boise's first recorded baseball game, the Hawks again won the Northwest League championship. They took two straight from the Bellingham Mariners in the playoffs. Individual stars were Mark Simmons at second base who hit .304, Jamie Burke, third base, .301, and David Kennedy, first base, who led the Hawks with 49 runs batted in. Brian Harris led the pitchers with 105 innings pitched, 96 strikeouts, an 8-2 record and an ERA of 1.89. Willard Brown pitched 83-2/3 innings, struck out 68, and held opponents to a .211 average.

Top: Phil Leftwich.
Bottom: Billy Hathaway.

Statesman photographer Troy Maben got this great action shot as Bend's Jerry Schoen scores. Elgin Bobo is the Boise catcher. June 16, 1991.

Acknowledgments I am indebted to many people for assistance over the years this study was in preparation. I especially appreciate the early encouragement and significant contributions of William S. Campbell, a longtime supporter of professional baseball in Boise. Gary L. Quigley generously shared much statistical information that he had accumulated.

Former colleagues and friends at the Idaho State Historical Society Library and Archives were unfailingly helpful and patient: Guila Ford, Elizabeth Jacox, Tomas Jaehn and John Yandell. I also appreciate the courteous assistance of William J. Wilson and Holly Huff at Boise Public Library and Elaine Leppert at Caldwell Public Library.

It was my great pleasure to spend many hours with former baseball players in this valley, sometimes with a tape recorder, sometimes in telephone conversations. Those who shared anecdotes, scrapbooks and photographs that greatly enriched the project were: Gerry Craft, Emil Drzayich, Bob King, Jeff Kollman, Walter A. Lowe, Jim Lyke, Tom Matsumoto, Ray Odermott, John E. Rasor, Paul Sereduk, Ned Sheehan, Bill Wigle and Gordon Williamson. Family members of players and officials also contributed generously with anecdotes, photos and scrapbooks: LaVonne Cummings, daughter of Mr. and Mrs. Ed Turnbaugh, John P. Halliwell, Jr., Mrs. Andrew Harrington, Anita Nishioka, Alice Nishitani and Carmen Urlezaga Subisarreta.

I also appreciate the contributions of Jeanette Anderson, Karl B. Brooks, Dorothy Chester, Mary. d'Easum, Nick Gill, Jerome Lester, Harold Southworth, James R. Simpson, Lorene Thurston and Philo West.

The fine photographs of the Boise Hawks are from the files of the *Idaho Statesman,* and are used with permission, as is some material first published there in my weekly newspaper column. The bulk of my research on Boise's long baseball history was done in the microfilmed files of the *Idaho Statesman,* published continuously since 1864.

Without a generous grant from West One Bank this book could not have been published in this format for release in 1994. The help of Jack P. Rucker, Vice President and Market Manager is gratefully acknowledged.

And last, again my appreciation to my wife, Novella Dee, for her willing and capable assistance in almost all aspects of this books's production.

ARTHUR A. HART

Index

Photo Credits

Caldwell Public Library, 20,40,61; William S. Campbell, 80,81,89A; Gerry Craft, 95; Mrs. C.G. d'Easum, 64; Emil Drzayich, 94,96; John P. Halliwell, Jr., 86,89B,90,91; Mrs. Andrew M. Harrington, 37,47,71,73A,74,75B; Idaho State Historical Society, 9,10,11,16,17,18,21,23,24,26,27,29,35,36,51,56,85; *Idaho Statesman*, 45,98,101,102A-B,103A-C; Lester Jerome, 78; Walter A. Lowe, 75A,87,88; Alice Nishitani, 65,66,67; Paul Sereduk, 76,77; Carmen Urlezaga Subisarreta, 63,68,70,72; Washington County Economic Development Commission, 33; Weiser Signal-American, 25; Dr. Gordon Williamson, 73B.